T0330570

Custom Kanban

Designing the System to Meet the
Needs of Your Environment

Raymond S. Louis

CRC Press
Taylor & Francis Group
Boca Raton London New York

CRC Press is an imprint of the
Taylor & Francis Group, an **informa** business

A PRODUCTIVITY PRESS BOOK

CRC Press
Taylor & Francis Group
6000 Broken Sound Parkway NW, Suite 300
Boca Raton, FL 33487-2742

© 2006 by Replenishment Technology Group, Inc.
CRC Press is an imprint of Taylor & Francis Group

No claim to original U.S. Government works
Printed in the United States of America on acid-free paper
10 9 8 7 6 5 4 3 2
International Standard Book Number-13: 978-1-56327-345-2 (Hardcover)
Library of Congress catalog number: 2006023556

Library of Congress Cataloging-in-Publication Data

Catalog record is available from the Library of Congress

Visit the Taylor & Francis Web site at
http://www.taylorandfrancis.com

and the CRC Press Web site at
http://www.crcpress.com

TABLE OF CONTENTS

CONTENTS

ACKNOWLEDGMENTS

To my wife, Laurie: Thank you for reviewing the entire book to ensure that I communicated clearly. Thanks are also due my colleagues Paul McGrath, Scott Myers, Brett Card, and Charles Louis, who reviewed key portions of the text, offering their insights and recommendations. Their input was valuable and appreciated. I am grateful to Maura May and Michael Sinocchi of Productivity Press, who accepted this work, and Tere Stouffer, freelance project editor, who developed the book's content, copyedited the text, and enhanced its presentation. Thanks are also due to Mary Junewick, who helped critique the initial work of the book's development.

PREFACE

K anban may be the simplest replenishment system to understand conceptually, and yet it is the most complex to apply successfully. This is not the fault of the practitioner or of the kanban methodology; it is due, instead, to the oversimplification of most literature that portrays kanban as a one-size-fits-all application that is, at best, a visual rendering. The literature does not deal with the complexities faced by the practitioner in applying this powerful tool to his or her specific environment. The typical portrayal usually demonstrates the final product being loaded smoothly and placed in a build sequence, several supporting part numbers hand-calculated and placed on a multiple container kanban option, triggered demand being presented to the source of replenishment in the form of kanban cards, and suppliers performing milk runs. For those who apply this vision as a literal kanban design to their specific environment, the reality is typically as follows:

- The final product build schedule cannot be loaded smoothly or sequenced to its fullest extent in most environments, and in a number of applications, not at all. This creates nonlinear demand patterns that will result in stockouts unless specific kanban techniques are applied.
- Not all part numbers can or should be placed on kanban due to their individual component profile, such as erratic demand patterns, quality issues, phase ins and phase outs, or supplier unwillingness to participate on kanban. For these and other reasons, a parallel alternative replenishment methodology is required for these part numbers, and their requirements must be in sync with the timing and quantities of kanban, when triggered.
- The supply base is typically not located within a short distance from the plant permitting milk runs. In fact, the majority of OEMs have supply bases spanning the North American continent and the globe.

- Other kanban container options other than the multiple container option are available and may be better suited for your specific component profile or environmental factors, permitting a least-total-cost solution from a transportation-inventory-carrying-cost standpoint.
- You may have too many part numbers to be effectively recalculated by hand each time the anticipated demand is projected to shift. Many environments have hundreds, thousands, and tens of thousands of part numbers. If the kanban lot sizes are not recalculated and adjusted immediately after demand shifts, stockouts will occur as well as inflated inventory. This may require automated kanban calculations.
- The amount of time and effort in many environments to manually adjust the number of kanban cards in process can be an overwhelming task, with each planning period depending on the quantity of part numbers and degree of shift in demand. Automated adjustments to the number of kanban cards or kanban lot sizes may be mandatory.
- In the world of collaborative supply chain, where the pull methodology is an integral component, it is difficult (if not impossible) to visualize multiple partners hand-calculating and phoning in collaborative information, such as projected demand or triggered requirements on thousands of part numbers. These systems are, more often than not, automated.

The most probable impact from a kanban design that is not suited for your environment is high inventory coupled with shortages, a triggering mechanism that is augmented by hot lists, late customer orders, and high operating costs from not eliminating the non-value-added activities associated with perpetuating the kanban system.

The manner in which your kanban system is implemented also plays a key role. An improperly implemented kanban system can have both immediate and long-term effects. An immediate impact could be as simple as mass shortages from implementing the lower level of components first while still batch building at the final assembly level. An example of a long-term effect of an improperly implemented kanban system is placing items on kanban that are too erratic in demand. These items would create stockouts well beyond the point of implementation and give the impression that safety stock needs to be increased on kanban items across the board when, in fact, only those items with erratic demand patterns need to be placed on alternative replenishment methodologies.

Kanban is a powerful technique. When designed and implemented correctly for the environment it is intended to serve, it becomes a highly competitive strategy. It operates so smoothly that a plant visitor will know it is effective but would be unaware of the kanban techniques that were selected to complement the specific environment. The real power behind the successful application of kanban is in understanding your environment, choosing kanban techniques that align with your environment, and implementing the system in a correct manner.

In over eighteen years of designing and implementing both manual and fully automated kanban for companies ranging in size from $12 million to $10 billion, Replenishment Technology Group (RTG) has identified twenty-five different design options. These design options are decision points within the kanban design process, at which specific kanban techniques are selected based on the environmental factors of the given company. Replenishment Technology Group has also taught kanban to hundreds of Fortune 500 manufacturing companies and has authored two books: *Kanban for American Industry* and *Integrating Kanban with MRPII* (Productivity Press). Replenishment Technology Group is fully aware of the industry diversity and the environmental differences that can exist, even between competitors building the same type of product.

The key to having a highly effective kanban system comes from it being designed to meet the specific needs of the environment it is intended to serve—and for it to be properly implemented. An effective kanban system does not come from replicating what was seen on a plant tour or by following overly simplistic kanban publications and workshops. Think of an airplane: You understand that an airplane has an engine, wings, and rudder, and can stay aloft, but it doesn't necessarily follow that you know how to build and fly the airplane.

The first objective of this book is to aid the practitioner in designing the kanban system, which entails selecting appropriate kanban techniques based on the specific environmental factors of your company. Environmental factors are the key characteristics of a company, and include customer expectations versus manufacturing response capability, linearity of customer demand, quantity of active part numbers, and the location and capabilities of suppliers. These and many other environmental factors dictate the specific kanban techniques that must be employed to meet the needs of the environment.

The second objective of this book is to offer guidance on the key aspects of successfully implementing kanban.

Chapter 1 provides an overview of kanban design and implementation. Chapters 2 through 7 deal specifically with the design of the kanban system. Each of these chapters represents a key kanban design category. These design categories are key functional *components* of kanban, that, when blended together, create a kanban *system*. Each design category has one or more *design options*, which are specific points within the category where the selection of kanban technique(s) must take place. Each kanban technique presented includes a description of the environment it is intended to serve. You then select the technique for consideration if the environment described matches your own environment. For example, Chapter 2 presents the design category of final product build strategy. One of the design options in this chapter is Design Option 1: Planning and initiating final product build. Within that design option, there are six specific kanban techniques from which to choose, based on the description of the environment the kanban technique is designed to serve. If a particular environment matches your environment, you should consider its associated technique for application. Twenty-five design options are covered within this text.

The intent of this book is to cover the design options and not necessarily to cover kanban basics. However, an appendix is provided to help the beginner with key basic subject areas, when they are brought up in discussion within the text. Segmenting the basics to the appendix permits concentration on the design options within the chapters while still providing the required information of the basics for the beginner. Finally, Chapter 8 deals with the implementation of the kanban system. Highly detailed, this chapter specifies each step of the kanban implementation process.

In addition, the intent of this book is to provide guidance to the reader as to the design options, diversification of environments, and the specific kanban techniques that should be considered for application and implementation. Understand that a book can go only so far in imparting knowledge; the balance depends on the skill level and due diligence of the practitioner. As with any technique or approach, nothing should be applied to any facility unless it is thoroughly understood and manually tested. At a minimum, this text is meant to enlighten the reader as to the design options and the interrelationship between the kanban techniques available and the environmental conditions they were designed to accommodate. In the hands of a cross-functional team of skilled practitioners applying due diligence, this text can be used to design and implement a world-class replenishment system. This text provides detail so that you may fully understand the design and implementation methodology and then program highly effective routines to apply to your environment, where appropriate. From a commercial standpoint, however, a number of Replenishment Technology Group, Inc.'s patents protect this work.

There are many more environments in existence than could ever be condensed into a single work. This text presents the most prevalent environments.

CHAPTER 1

KANBAN DESIGN AND IMPLEMENTATION OVERVIEW

The process of implementing kanban typically begins with a vision. The vision is paramount in initiating action, but the action should not be *implementation* but rather *understanding* your environmental needs, fully designing a kanban system intended to serve those environmental needs, and then implementing the system in a correct manner.

The Kanban Vision

When touring a plant that has a highly effective kanban system, the system appears simplistic and self-perpetuating. Employees are not running around with hot lists, the production process is efficient, and the plant seems almost void of material. When the host is questioned concerning the kanban system, the response reinforces what the visiting team has already read concerning kanban. A predetermined quantity is kept on hand, consumption triggers replenishment, suppliers respond to the plant replenishment needs, and the benefits are enormous. When the tour is concluded, the team is excited about applying kanban to their plant. The vision is quite clear.

However, what typically is not available from the tour or in most publications is that no two kanban systems are identical and what was seen cannot in its entirety be emulated. More importantly, what was not seen or explained is quite extensive. In other words, the key to having an effective kanban system begins with understanding the needs of your specific environment, and then applying the appropriate kanban techniques to satisfy those needs. Equally as important is how kanban is implemented. Regardless of how

1

effectively the kanban system is designed, an improperly implemented kanban system can create immediate problems. Some aspects of an improperly implemented kanban system can keep the system ineffective long after the implementation has taken place.

Typical Outcome of a Proper Kanban Design

A properly designed kanban system will be tailored to meet the needs of the environment and will encounter minimal issues on a day-to-day basis. (See Figure 1-1.) The rewards for properly designing and implementing a kanban system are enormous. A well-designed kanban system can provide what is needed, when needed, in appropriate quantities, while significantly lowering inventory, shortages, non-value-added activities, and total overall costs. Customer on-time deliveries are dramatically improved, while the overall quality of life for the organization is enhanced immensely, permitting concentration on strategic matters rather than continuously compensating for an ineffective replenishment system. With proper kanban design and implementation, the system will, at

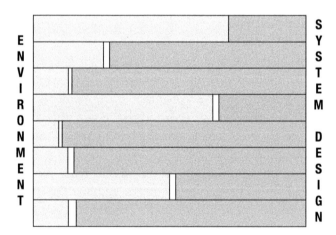

Each bar of the kanban system design represents a kanban technique selected by the team to meet the needs of the environment.

Figure 1-1. Design of the kanban system that meets the needs of the environment.

a minimum, match that of any competitor and, in application, appear to perpetuate itself without effort.

Impact of an Improper Kanban Design

This text has twenty-five kanban design options for which environmental factors are evaluated and kanban techniques selected. Working together, the kanban techniques selected form an overall kanban system that meets the needs of the environment, as demonstrated in Figure 1-1. Each bar represents a kanban technique selected. The end result of the kanban technique(s) selected defines a kanban system meant to satisfy the needs of your specific environment. The symptoms of an improperly designed kanban system are high inventory levels coupled with shortages, triggered containers not having credibility due to inflated kanban lot sizes, hot lists, increased total costs, and late customer orders. This is a direct result of not tailoring the kanban system to meet the needs of the environment it is intended to serve. (See Figure 1-2.) High inventory levels are normally a result of high safety-stock settings

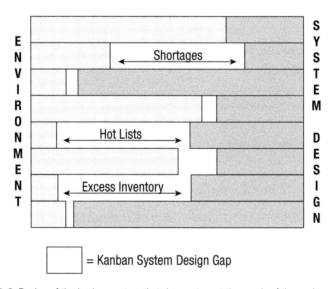

☐ = Kanban System Design Gap

Figure 1-2. Design of the kanban system that does not meet the needs of the environment.

compensating for the misgivings of the kanban system design. Hot lists emerge due to the lack of credibility of the triggering process; after all, there is typically plenty of material left in all the other untriggered containers. While it may be true that a company can state that it is officially on kanban, it does not change the fact that the kanban system in question is only a shadow of its overall potential. In rare cases, users may be better off with their improperly designed kanban system than they were previously and may believe that life is currently good. The analogy would be similar to a person crossing the desert barefooted who is given cardboard soles. The cardboard may be hailed as a miracle, but it does not lend itself to competing in a marathon. Today, with global competition, each company is in a marathon to become and remain the absolute best in the world.

Kanban Design Categories

The kanban system in this text is divided into six design categories. Each design category performs a key function of the kanban system. Within each design category are specific unique design options. The design options are decision points within the design category where various kanban techniques are presented and selected based on the environmental factors of the business. The kanban techniques selected for each design category work together to perform the design category function in a specific manner. When the six design categories are blended together, what emerges is a kanban system designed for your specific environment. These kanban design categories are briefly discussed in the following sections.

Final Product Build Strategy (Chapter 2)

A manufacturer would find it difficult to remain profitable if it allowed its production volume to swing erratically. To control the linearity of demand, a final product build strategy needs to be implemented. The objectives of the final product build strategy are to linearize production while satisfying customer delivery expectations. Without a linear demand pattern, kanban would be ineffective to the degree of nonlinearity. Environmental factors include the linearity of customer demand and customer expectations versus manufacturing/delivery capability. This chapter also discusses forecasts that, for most environments, play a vital role in projecting anticipated demand quantities used in the construction of the master production schedule, which provides the foundation for capacity planning, supplier projections, and calculating kanban lot sizes. Environmental factors dictating the kanban technique employed in forecasting include the quantity of forecasted items and the repeatability of history. The key is to develop and utilize the forecast before the change in demand impacts the environment.

Kanban Lot Size Calculation (Chapter 3)

There are numerous environmental factors that go beyond the basic formula that dictate the kanban lot size. This includes such fundamental environmental factors as setup time issues, transportation costs, item costs, and suppliers' minimums and multiples. Going one step further, linearity of demand is crucial. The kanban lot size calculation must take into consideration nonlinear demand patterns; if not, stockouts will occur to the degree it exists and is ignored. In joint environments where material requirement planning (MRP) items and kanban items coexist, the MRP items that go into kanban items must know the precise timing and quantities of what will be triggered so that they can be supported. This requires a Synchronized Explosion™ with simulation capability. This is demonstrated so that the reader can be alerted to program this capability (according to the material described in this text, if it pertains to them).

Kanban Containers, Triggering, and Maintenance (Chapter 4)

There are numerous container options, each designed to accommodate specific environmental factors. These environmental factors include supplier distance from the plant, size and weight of parts, their cost, ability to perpetuate inventory accurately, transportation costs, and demand volume. Kanban-triggering techniques are also selected based on environmental factors, such as quantity of part numbers on kanban, distance of suppliers, whether or not there are MRP items in the environment, whether the environment is labor intensive, and the size of the plant. The manner in which triggering takes place determines other capabilities. If dealing with hundreds and thousands of part numbers, the triggered data needs to be in the computer so that each work cell can see the actual triggered load and cross-trained personnel can be shifted to where the load resides, suppliers can download the trigger demand, and MRP items sharing the same resource as kanban items can be blended together. The maintenance of adding and subtracting the number of cards in play can be automatically adjusted if dealing with hundreds and thousands of kanban items. The proper selection of techniques determines the response capability, accuracy, indirect costs, and effectiveness of the organization. Lack of capabilities in the environment that require them would seriously impair the speed and effectiveness of reaction to demand. The analogy would be like having a giant ship improperly designed with a small rudder.

Receiving, Inspection, Shipping, and Material Handling (Chapter 5)

You must have a *least total cost* mindset when selecting the kanban techniques for receiving, inspection, shipping, and material handling. A company can overwhelm itself with indirect costs, while achieving minimal reductions in inventory levels. Environmental factors such as unit costs and associated volume, critical and noncritical components, and volume of items on kanban must be taken into consideration when selecting the appropriate kanban techniques.

Operating Kanban in Manufacturing (Chapter 6)

How kanban drives and supports manufacturing is vital, and the design of the kanban system that operates kanban in manufacturing is also dependent on environmental factors. These environmental factors include predictability of demand, the quantity of part numbers that make up a subassembly/assembly or final product, and the degree of labor required to make the triggered item. The environment determines the order in which triggered items should be produced, whether material simulations for availability of supporting material should take place prior to releasing the triggered item for production, and whether current triggered load reflecting hours of work should be made available to shift cross-trained production personnel. If the kanban techniques do not match the environment, you will find it nearly impossible to be fully aware of what is occurring in order to respond effectively.

Operating Kanban with Suppliers (Chapter 7)

It is often in the OEM's best interest to consolidate the supply base, where the benefits come in the form of lower overall negotiated price, supplier willingness to participate in kanban, and a working relationship that is groomed into a partnership. How the consolidation is approached depends on the environmental factors of the items being purchased. There is a distinct difference in technique if the items being consolidated are commodity off-the-shelf items or company-designed items. The improper technique applied in consolidating the supply base can have serious consequences. For a supplier to be effective, it needs projections of anticipated demand to plan capacity, and it may be required to carry the lead-time quantity based on the environmental factors of past supplier performance. Supplier interface is also all important in today's supply chains. Environmental factors such as the quantity of part numbers on kanban and the distance of suppliers dictates the kanban techniques that are used to interface.

Kanban Implementation

Implementation plays a vital role, because it can either impair or complement the selected kanban techniques. For example, items with erratic demand patterns that are selected for kanban can create stockouts, regardless of how well the kanban system is designed.

The same can be said for numerous other factors, such as placing suppliers on kanban who have a history of quality and delivery problems or placing components onto kanban that have an exceptionally long lead time, creating an inflation of inventory. Chapter 8 covers the fourteen steps to implementing kanban internally and externally to the plant. Topics covered in that chapter are briefly discussed in the following sections.

Sequence of Implementation

The fourteen steps are presented in the order in which kanban should be implemented. Each step is discussed in detail, permitting an understanding of why these steps are necessary, along with examples where applicable.

Selection Process of Part Numbers to Place on Kanban

Not all part numbers can or should be on kanban. You must establish a selection criterion that identifies the appropriate characteristics of kanban candidates. One example is the degree of linearity of the item being considered for kanban. Placing components on kanban that have erratic demand patterns will continue to negatively affect your business long after the implementation has taken place.

Determination of Safety-Stock Levels and Techniques for Determining Anticipated Inventory Levels

Chapter 8 shows you how to assess the linearity of demand, how to determine the degree of safety stock required, and how to determine your anticipated average inventory levels if these items are placed on kanban as they compare to current inventory levels.

Supplier Key Considerations

You will need to take a number of items into consideration when implementing kanban with the supply base. This includes key measurements that can let you know whether the kanban system is not reducing inventory as was projected and see supplier performance ratings that enable early detection and correction of supplier performance issues. Also covered are key items that should be stated in the supplier contract.

General Guidelines for Selecting Kanban Techniques

Keep in mind two basic concepts beyond environmental factors when selecting kanban techniques throughout this book. The first general concept is that a technique can be applied broadly to the plant as a whole or can pertain to specific part numbers. For example, when determining the kanban lot size calculation design option, if a plant has 12,000 part numbers on kanban and the projected anticipated demand changes monthly and experiences nonlinear demand patterns, the technique of *automated recalculation* would be selected versus *manual recalculation*. This particular technique is applied broadly throughout the plant for items selected as kanban items. To demonstrate a part-by-part determination of a kanban technique, consider kanban containers. For example, some part numbers may require a *multiple container* technique because the sheer volume and size of the components necessitate that approach, while much smaller components of a lesser volume and close supply source may necessitate a dual container application. From these two examples, you can see plant-wide technique and a technique that is applied on a part-by-part basis.

The second concept is that any automated kanban technique selected must have a *payback*. The kanban techniques outlined in this book include manual and automated methodologies. The environmental factors are quite clear in guiding the selection. For automated kanban techniques, however, it is important to understand a basic guideline when it comes to non-value-added activities. For manufacturers to respond rapidly and effectively to customer demand at the least total cost, non-value-added activities must be eliminated or streamlined from the manufacturing processes and the replenishment system. By definition, all activity associated with any replenishment system is considered non-value-added, because it does not physically transform, convert, or change the shape of the product for customer use. The goal during the design process is to eliminate or automate each manual activity associated with it while retaining or developing the ability to obtain what is needed, when needed, and in the appropriate quantities. At the same time, there must be a payback for any element of lean manufacturing implemented, and kanban is no exception. This is not a paradox but rather a premise for selecting the appropriate kanban technique for your specific environment. Stated differently, one of the kanban design goals is to eliminate the non-value-added activities, but it must have a payback. For example, after recalculating kanban lot sizes, the number of kanban cards for the multiple container application must be added and subtracted. There is a manual method of gathering the excess cards and distributing the cards that are to be added. If your environment has several thousand part numbers on kanban employing the multiple bin container option with demand fluctuating from one planning period to the next, the process of adding and subtracting cards can be overwhelming from both a labor and response time standpoint. Consideration should be given to automating this function. If, on the other hand, the projected demand rarely changes or if you are dealing with a only small quantity of part numbers (for example, 100) you may wish to use a manual method of adding and subtracting kanban cards as opposed to allocating resources to automate the process. Although adding and subtracting kanban cards is a non-value-added activity, in this example there would be little payback in the time and expenditure for automating the adjustment of kanban cards when so little time would be devoted to that particular activity.

Conclusion

The intent of this book is to provide guidance to the reader on the diverse environments and the specific kanban techniques that should be considered for application. It should be understood that a book can go only so far in imparting knowledge; the balance depends on the skill level and due diligence of the practitioner. As with any technique or approach, nothing should be applied to any facility unless it is thoroughly understood and tested. To begin this process, we move to Chapter 2, where we cover the first of six kanban design categories: final product build strategy.

FINAL PRODUCT BUILD STRATEGY

A manufacturer would find it difficult to remain profitable if it allowed its production volume to swing erratically. The typical impact would include:

- Quality issues exist, such as temporary untrained workers brought in to deal with peak loads and regular employees creating errors due to excessive overtime.
- Machine reliability would deteriorate due to lack of routine maintenance, creating work stoppages and quality issues.
- Lack of a predictability of product flow exists throughout the plant and supply chain, making it exceptionally difficult to give and meet accurate promise ship dates to customers.
- Excessive inventory is built up throughout the supply chain.
- Sales orders are delinquent.
- Overall costs are excessive, due to the accumulation of total supply-chain inefficiencies.

The end result is loss of customers due to high cost, poor quality, and on-time delivery issues. The importance of final-product build linearity cannot be overstated from an overall business standpoint. This is especially true when it comes to the application of kanban in the manufacturing arena, because kanban requires a linear demand pattern or the end result will be high inventory levels coupled with shortages. The degree to which additional costs and inefficiencies will occur from a nonlinear-demand manufacturing environment operating kanban is directly proportional to the degree of nonlinearity of the final build. The twofold objective is to satisfy customer demand within customer expectations, while ensuring a linear final product build exists. There are two design options that work in tandem in achieving the two objectives: Design Option 1 (Planning and Initiating Final Product Build) and Design Option 2 (Forecasts). We begin with Design Option 1.

Design Option 1: Planning and Initiating Final Product Build

Determining which technique(s) to employ to plan and initiate the final product build is predicated on the environmental factors of the business. Environmental factors include level of product standardization, linearity of customer demand, and customer delivery expectations as compared with manufacturing and delivery capability, and the ability of the manufacturing environment with regard to *one-piece flow*. The techniques employed for initiating the final product build can be a sequenced schedule; customer orders initiating the build directly to the final product line; triggering of finished goods kanban, initiating the build directly to the final product line; or the production line driven by a master production schedule. More than one technique may be employed within a plant, depending on the environmental factors of the individual final products.

Kanban Technique 1: Build to a Sequenced Schedule

A sequenced schedule (final assembly schedule) drives the final product build. (See Appendix A.)

Environmental Factors for Kanban Technique 1
- Standard product either has or does not have options.
- Customer demand is not linear.
- Manufacturing and delivery response capability is longer than customer expectation.
- Manufacturing has one-piece flow capability.

Application of Kanban Technique 1

A load-smooth master production schedule (see Appendix A) is made that encompasses current final product customer orders and forecast within capacity constraints. In its development, it also takes into consideration on-hand finished goods inventory. The load-smooth master production schedule takes place in the early planning stages, and sequencing takes place within a short period prior to production, as customer orders can replace forecast where applicable. Sequencing is updated each day, at a minimum. The build on the final product assembly line or work cell can be controlled via a Heijunka box (see Appendix A), which contains final assembly sequenced cards or is automated, employing a computer monitor and printer at the head of the production line.

The following factors create a one-piece flow capability that permits a build to a sequenced schedule:

- Flexible work cells can add or subtract workers as the demand fluctuates.
- Flexible workforce is able to work in a number of different work cells.
- Manufacturing is able to perform rapid changeovers on machines.
- Manufacturing maintains excess capacity to handle fluctuations.
- Mistake-proofing is employed, permitting quality to be produced at the source.
- Total Productive Maintenance (TPM) is applied to ensure peak performance and uptime of machines.
- Main suppliers are within a short distance of the plant and/or employ a common warehouse.

The load-smooth master production schedule will drive the bill of material explosion used in calculating lower-level kanban lot sizes (where applicable), determine internal capacity requirements, and provide visibility of anticipated demand to the supply base. The supply base will predicate its delivery based on triggered kanban for kanban items and/or a downloaded sequenced schedule on selected items.

Key Notes

1. *Finished goods inventory is required to smooth production.*
2. *Finished goods may be necessary at distribution points and dealerships for high-volume finished goods items if customer expectations are not being met due to customer distance issues.*

Kanban Technique 2: Build to Customer Orders

Customer orders initiate the build directly to the final product assembly line or work cell.

Environmental Factors for Kanban Technique 2

- Standard products have or do not have options.
- Customer demand is linear.
- Manufacturing/delivery response capability is within customer expectation.
- Manufacturing has a one-piece flow capability.

Application of Kanban Technique 2

As customer bookings occur, they are transmitted directly to the final assembly line or work cell that is responsible for production of the final product. Finished goods inventory is not maintained.

A load-smooth master production schedule is made, encompassing current final product customer orders and forecast within capacity constraints, and is used for planning purposes only. In its construction, there is no finished goods inventory to take into consideration, as it is not maintained. The load-smooth master production schedule will drive the bill of material explosion used in calculating lower-level kanban lot sizes where applicable, determine internal capacity requirements, and provide visibility of anticipated demand to the supply base. The supply base will predicate its delivery depending on triggered kanban for kanban items.

Kanban Technique 3: Combination; Build to Triggered Kanban and Customer Orders

For high-volume final product, kanban is maintained, and consumption through customer orders triggers replenishment on the final assembly line or work cell. For low-volume final product, there is no finished goods inventory, and the final product build is initiated directly by customer demand to the final assembly line or work cell.

Environmental Factors for Kanban Technique 3

- Standard product has or does not have options.
- Customer demand is linear on high-volume products and erratic on low-volume products.
- The current manufacturing and delivery response capability is longer than customer expectation.
- Manufacturing has a one-piece flow capability.

Application of Kanban Technique 3

Customer bookings for standard high-volume product items are satisfied directly from the finished goods kanban inventory, which is on kanban. This satisfies customer expectations, as it is readily available. When consumption occurs, a replenishment order is triggered directly to the final assembly line or work cell responsible for replenishment. Customer orders for standard low-volume product are satisfied directly from the final assembly line or work cell responsible for manufacturing and given priority over standard high-volume products, enabling turnaround within customer delivery expectation. A load-smooth master production schedule for kanban final product items is constructed for this environment, encompassing customer orders and forecast within capacity constraints, and is used for planning purposes. The master production schedule for low-volume items reflects customer orders as well as forecasts, which may be predicated on historical information or current marketing information. The master production schedule will be used to calculate final product kanban lot sizes of high-volume product, drive the bill of material explosion used in calculating lower-level kanban lot sizes (where applicable), determine internal capacity requirements, and provide visibility of anticipated demand to the supply base. The supply base will predicate its delivery depending on triggered kanban for kanban items.

Key Notes

1. *Low-volume final product is not kept on the shelf as a kanban item, because its demand pattern is often erratic. To build and maintain the safety stock required to prevent stockouts would create the opportunity for obsolescence. Unless they are common items, the unique supporting assemblies, subassemblies, components, and material associated with low-volume final product have erratic demand patterns and may not be good candidates for kanban.*

2. *By giving low-volume standard products priority on the production line or work cell, their lead time is only a fraction of that of standard high-volume products. The majority of manufacturing lead time, typically 90 percent, is queue time. Reducing the queue time helps bring the manufacturing lead time within range of customer delivery expectations. The high-volume standard product is readily available on the finished goods shelf and has minimal risk of becoming obsolete.*

3. *If customer orders for low-volume standard products do not materialize as forecasted within a short period prior to production, they are dropped from the master production schedule and are not built.*

4. *Finished goods may be necessary at distribution points and dealerships for high-volume finished goods items if customer expectations are not being met due to customer distance issues.*

Kanban Technique 4: Combination; Build to Master Production Schedule and Customer Orders

For high-volume standard product, a master production schedule is used to drive the final product build at the final assembly line or work cell. For low-volume standard product, the final product build is initiated directly by customer orders to the final assembly line or work cell. Finished goods inventory is built and placed on the shelf for high-volume standard product, as required for level loading the shop. Finished goods inventory is not built for low-volume standard product.

Environmental Factors for Kanban Technique 4

- Standard products do or do not have options.
- Customer demand is erratic or seasonal.
- The current manufacturing and delivery response capability is longer than customers' expectations.
- Finished goods build requires lot sizing.

Application of Kanban Technique 4

A master production schedule is made, taking into consideration capacity, current customer orders, forecasted orders for both high- and low-volume finished goods items, current finished goods inventory, and the requirement to level load the shop, utilizing a buildup or decrease of high-volume finished goods. When customer demand is expected to be low, high-volume finished goods inventory will increase. When customer demand is expected to be high, the high-volume finished goods inventory will decrease. Low-volume products are not kept in finished goods and, as bookings occur, are satisfied directly from the final-product production line or work cell and given priority-enabling turnaround within customer expectations. This master production schedule is lot-sized, as required to match the capabilities of the final assembly line or work cell, and takes into consideration the degree of finished goods inventory that will be generated in order to linearize the build and satisfy customer expectations. Final product lot sizing is key when calculating kanban lot sizes for the supporting items, because the lower-level kanban lot size calculations must take into consideration the nonlinear demand patterns occurring at the upper level; otherwise, stockouts will occur. This lot-sized master production schedule will be used to calculate lower-level kanban lot sizes, determine internal capacity requirements, and provide visibility of anticipated demand to the supply base. The supply base will predicate its delivery depending on triggered demand for kanban items.

Key Notes

1. *The lot-sized master production schedule will be used by the final-product assembly line or work cell in directing what is built for high-volume standard final product.*
2. *Forecasted low-volume standard product reflected on the lot-sized master production schedule is used only for planning purposes.*
3. *Finished goods may be necessary at distribution points and dealerships for high-volume finished goods items if customer expectations are not being met due to customer distance issues.*

Kanban Technique 5: Build to Customer Specifications on Basic Models

Customer orders initiate the final product build. A master production schedule encompassing customer orders and planning numbers (forecast) that are based on planned capacity per time period is used to linearize the final product build.

Environmental Factors for Kanban Technique 5

- Standard final product is highly customized per customer specification(s).
- Customer demand is not linear.
- Manufacturing and delivery response capability is within customer expectation.
- The manufacturing environment requires various degrees of lot sizing.

Application of Kanban Technique 5

Customer orders drive the final product build. Available capacity is used to control the booking process in regard to what products can be promised by specific time periods. This produces a master production schedule that is reasonably load-smooth from a capacity utilization standpoint. The master production schedule is made up of booked customer orders and forecasted orders by product type, quantity, and time period. There are no finished goods in this environment. Each forecasted product type on the master production schedule is represented by a *planning number*, which is backed by planning bills of material (e.g., modular bills of material or pseudo bills of material). The planning numbers are not produced at the final product level but are reserved seats for customer orders when booked. The planning bills of material attached to the planning numbers contain a standard list of assemblies, subassemblies, components, and raw material that are used to build a specific model. It is not a complete list of all the items used, because the balance will be defined when an order is booked as the OEM engineers work with the customer to further define the product specifications. When a customer order is being booked, the order desk will look for an unreserved "seat" in the load-smooth master production schedule. Once an unreserved seat is located, the planning number is removed and is replaced with the actual final product part number. The unreserved seat in actuality is a forecast and is used as a tool to linearize the final product build via a rough-cut capacity plan (the intent is to linearize the production load); it is also used as a vehicle to plan lower-level standard items. If an unreserved seat is not filled within a specific lead time from the final assembly start date, the unreserved seat is discarded. The load-smooth master production schedule is exploded, providing the basis from which to calculate lower-level kanban lot sizes (where kanban is applicable), determine internal capacity requirements, and provide visibility of anticipated demand to the supply base. The supply base will predicate its delivery based on triggered demand for kanban items. Kanban is an important tool, because maintaining a predetermined quantity of on-hand inventory on commonly used items helps shorten the response lead time to the customer.

Kanban Technique 6: Make to Order

Customer orders initiate the final product build. A master production schedule is constructed, encompassing current bookings, and is interfaced with the material requirements planning module, shop scheduling module, and capacity planning module. Capacity versus current load, coupled with lead time considerations, dictate the commit date as customer orders are being booked, and this is the prime tool in keeping the shop linear. Kanban may be applied at the lower levels due to a high degree of commonality (e.g., assemblies, subassemblies, raw material).

Environmental Factors for Kanban Technique 6

- The operation is a job shop.
- Customer demand is not linear.
- Specific unit demand cannot be forecasted; dollars by time period can be forecasted.
- There is a high degree of commonality at the lower levels.
- The current manufacturing and delivery response capability is within customer expectations.

Application of Kanban Technique 6

Lower-level items, such as raw materials with a high degree of commonality, may be placed on kanban and be highly effective in reducing inventory while minimizing overall customer lead time due to the material being on hand as bookings occur. Typically, historical usage at the raw material level is picked up from the computer system, manipulated based upon anticipated dollar shipment levels, and used to calculate kanban lot sizes. This process is covered in Chapter 3.

Design Option 2: Generating the Forecast

A *forecast* is typically required to provide information from which to create the master production schedule. The sales and marketing team typically is responsible for constructing the sales forecast. In a number of environments, this task is fairly complex and time consuming. Often, the change in what is being booked is upon the business *prior* to the development, publication, and application of the new forecast. In addition, for a number of environments, the completed forecast is not in a usable state from which to construct a master production schedule, because the forecast is expressed in dollars by product code and must therefore endure further delays in making the translation into units. In this section, we look into the design options of generating a forecast.

Kanban Technique 1: Timely Ready-to-Use Forecast

Sales and marketing provides a forecast reflecting final product part number, quantity, and time period. The forecast is used in constructing the master production schedule or is used in determining the final product stocking levels for the distribution centers.

Environmental Factors for Kanban Technique 1

- Standard products
- Small quantity of final product, with the forecast stated in terms of final product number, quantity, and time period
- Forecast readily available without delay

Application of Kanban Technique 1

The forecast is applied immediately in the construction of the master production schedule or in the determination of stocking levels of final product at the distribution centers.

Kanban Technique 2: Automated Forecast

Sales and marketing provides a forecast expressed in dollars, by time period, and by product code. Computerize a forecast routine utilizing historical data to translate the forecasted dollars into quantity of final product, by part number and by month.

Environmental Factors for Kanban Technique 2

- Standard products
- Hundreds or thousands of final product part numbers
- Historical sales data by product code in the computer, insofar as part number, quantity, and time period sold
- Historical mix within product code that repeats itself
- Sales price that may or may not change during the course of time

Application of Kanban Technique 2

Have the computer programmed to perform the following steps:

Step 1: The user will input a from date and a to date in the forecasting program, which tells the system how far into the past to go in picking up historical sales quantities of final product by part number and product code. The date selected must encompass full-month increments. For this example we have selected a "from" date of March 1, 2007 and a "to" date of May 31, 2007, a range that equals three full individual months: March, April, and May. (See Figure 2-1.) In this example, we see that Product Code 56, trench couplings, has three final product part numbers: 56-C, 56-D, and 56-E. The program will capture the quantity of units that were shipped for each month and extend those individual quantities times current unit price. The current unit price is $3.00 for 56-C, $5.00 for 56-D, and $20.00 for 56-E. From this example, we can also see that the total sales figure ($119,000 for March, $121,920 for April, and $123,700 for May) was determined, giving us a three-month historical sales average of $121,540 per month. The three-month average quantity of units sold equals 1,090 units for 56-C; 22,346 units for 56-D; and 327 units for 56-E.

June 1, 2007 Current Date
March 1, 2007 "From Date"
May 31, 2007 "To Date"

Product Code 56 Trench Couplings

Demand History

Model	March		April		May		3 Month Average	
	Units	Dollars	Units	Dollars	Units	Dollars	Units	Dollars
56-C	1,000	$3,000	1,100	$3,300	1,170	$3,510	1,090	$3,270
56-D	22,000	$110,000	22,400	$112,000	22,638	$113,190	22,346	$111,730
56-E	300	$6,000	331	$6,620	350	$7,000	327	$6,540
Total $	$119,000		$121,920		$123,700		$121,540 Average	

Figure 2-1. Historical sales averages calculated.

Step 2: The user will then key in the coming months' forecast dollars by product code. For our example, a sales forecast of $110,000 is forecasted for June, $120,000 for July, $130,000 for August, and $140,000 for September. (See Figure 2-2.) The program will then determine a *times factor* for each of the forecasted months, by dividing the forecasted dollar for each month by the three-month historical sales average of $121,540. For example, for June, we expect to ship $110,000, which we would divide by the $121,540 sales average to equal a times factor of 0.9050518. The program will repeat this routine for each month, as shown in Figure 2-2.

$121,540 Average Dollar Shipped: March–May				
Product Code 56 Trench Couplings				
Forecast/Times Factor Calculation				
	June	**July**	**August**	**September**
Dollar Forecast	$110,000	$120,000	$130,000	$140,000
Times Factor	0.9050518	0.9873292	1.0696067	1.1518841

Figure 2-2. Forecast and calculated times factor.

Step 3: Next, the program will multiply the times factor that was determined for each month times each final product part numbers' three-month unit average to determine the quantity of units forecasted. (See Figure 2-3.) For example, the times factor for June is 0.9050518, and it is first multiplied times final part number 56-C's three-month unit average of 1,090 units. This equals a June forecast of 987 units. Next, for the same month of June, the times factor is multiplied times final part number 56-D's three-month unit average of 22,346, to equal a June forecast of 20,224. Finally for the same month of June, the times factor is multiplied by final part number 56-E's three-month average of 327, to equal a June forecast of 296 units. Once the month of June is completed, the times factor for July is then multiplied times the three-month average for each final product, and so on. To demonstrate the accuracy of this method, we extend out all the final products units forecasted times the current

price by month, add up the extension, and compare it to the overall dollars forecasted for that specific month. For example, in Figure
2-3, the forecasted dollars for June was $110,000 for product code
56. As you can see, we were within $1 of the forecast due to round-
ing.

Step 4: The preceding process is repeated for each month of the
new forecast (this includes the product code for part sales, if applicable). Once the forecast is made, it is available for marketing/sales
review (via computer screen) and can be modified as required
based on specific customer information.

Key Notes

1. Additional capability can be added beyond Step 4, such as having each
   month's forecasted quantity divided by the number of manufacturing days
   in the month and automatically load the master production schedule, with
   a daily load-smooth forecast or lot sized based on typical run quantities
   required. Also, the program can automatically load the master production
   schedule with firm customer orders. This, of course, will be reviewed and
   modified by the master production scheduler as required.
2. If extremely large individual customer orders occur on occasion, they can
   be automatically removed by the program prior to being accounted for in
   Step 1 through a subroutine. This subroutine can first determine the average daily demand, and then, if the sales quantity is greater than XX days
   (a user input), the large individual customer orders will be omitted from
   being picked up and taken into consideration.
3. The automated forecasting methodology described in this section can be
   applied to the product code of spare sales. After the forecasted monthly
   quantities are determined, they are simply divided by the number of manufacturing days in each respective month to determine average daily
   demand and automatically load the master production schedule. This, of
   course, can be reviewed and modified by the master production scheduler, as required.
4. The automated forecasting methodology can also be used to calculate the
   average daily demand for final product for each distribution center. Sales

Product Code 56 Trench Couplings
Unit Forecast Calculation

Model	3 Month Unit Average	June 0.9050518 TF $110,000 Forecast		July 0.9873292 TF $120,000 Forecast		August 1.0696067 TF $130,000 Forecast		September 1.1518841 TF $140,000 Forecast	
		Units	Dollars	Units	Dollars	Units	Dollars	Units	Dollars
56-C	1,090	987	$2,961	1,076	$3,228	1,166	$3,498	1,256	$3,768
56-D	22,346	20,224	$101,120	22,063	$110,315	23,901	$119,505	25,740	$128,700
56-E	327	296	$5,920	323	$6,460	350	$7,000	377	$7,540
Total $ ⟶		$110,001		$120,003		$130,003		$140,008	

Figure 2-3. Calculating unit forecast.

and marketing would have to provide a dollar forecast for each distribution center, and the historical sales database would have to differentiate the sales in units that took place for each distribution center. The projected sales quantity for the month would then be divided by the number of days in the month to determine average daily demand. The average daily demand would then be applied to a formula to determine kanban lot sizes or min–max for each of the individual distribution centers.

It may seem like a lot of work to design and test your own forecast program, but it is nothing when compared to the monthly, repetitive, manual grind of performing this task. More importantly, automating the forecasting process will be more accurate than performing the math manually, and the automated forecasting can be done in a fraction of the time it takes to perform it manually, permitting a rapid response to projected shifts in demand.

Conclusion

The straightforward objective of a final product build strategy is to satisfy customer demand within customer expectations and linearize the final product build. Without linearity of demand, the kanban system will fail as a result of stockouts unless augmented by safety stock. Safety stock applied liberally will inflate inventory and create a credibility issue, with the kanban-triggering process resulting in the need for a hot list. Some of the issues creating nonlinearity at the final product level are self-inflicted, such as offering discounts for volume purchases or running special promotions. Other issues have more to do with environmental factors, such as having seasonal products or not having a broad base of customers. Whatever the root cause(s) of nonlinearity, it should not be accepted as a given and needs to be investigated and rectified if at all possible. In a number of cases, the root cause(s) can be rectified, providing a greater degree of linearity, which in turn permits a larger number of part numbers to be placed on kanban. Once the top-level demand patterns are investigated and corrected as much as possible, you should select from the kanban techniques discussed to plan and drive the final product build.

We discussed the need to generate a forecast, which is often a key component of the master production schedule. Some environments can create a forecast and enact it without delay, while others may have hundreds and even thousands of part numbers to forecast. In most cases, an automated methodology can be created, utilizing your current system, because the historical data, more often than not, already resides in your system. All you have to do is write and test the routines to automate the forecasting process and provide key review points and override capability. The benefit is accuracy in calculations and a rapid and effective means to respond to anticipated shifts in demand. The automated approach does not apply to every environment, but for those where it does, it can make a world of difference.

Now that we have selected the appropriate techniques to linearize and initiate final product production, we have the right forecasting tools available to aid us in effectively generating a master production schedule. We are now ready to begin calculating kanban lot sizes, covered in Chapter 3. You will discover that there is much more to determining kanban lot sizes than simply applying a formula.

KANBAN LOT SIZE CALCULATION

There are numerous kanban formulas, and they all contain the same basic elements as demonstrated in the following formula.

$$\frac{\text{(Average Daily Demand)} \times \text{(Replenishment Lead Time + Safety Stock)}}{\text{Standard Container Quantity}}$$

The replenishment lead time and safety stock are expressed as days or as a fraction of a day. The kanban lot size is the top part of the formula. Its quantity must be able to continue to support production, once a trigger occurs, until it is received and placed at the point of use. In the case of a multiple-container application, the kanban order quantity is the bottom portion of the formula. For the single discrete container, the kanban order quantity is one for one; for a single full container or dual/triple container, the kanban order quantity equals the full kanban lot size. The information is summarized as follows.

Container Type	Kanban Lot Size	Kanban Order Quantity
Multiple container	(average daily demand) × (replenishment lead time + safety stock)	Standard container quantity
Single container discrete	(average daily demand) × (replenishment lead time + safety stock)	One for one
Single container full	(average daily demand) × (replenishment lead time + safety stock)	Full kanban lot size
Dual container	(average daily demand) × (replenishment lead time + safety stock)	Full kanban lot size
Triple container	(average daily demand) × (replenishment lead time + safety stock)	Full kanban lot size

When demand is anticipated to change, the kanban lot sizes of purchased items and nonflexible work cell kanban items must have their kanban lot sizes recalculated and applied to the environment. A number of kanban techniques can be employed to perform the calculation of kanban lot sizes and the selection of the specific technique depends upon the environmental factors of the business. In this chapter we will demonstrate three diverse environments and then reflect the kanban techniques that should be considered for selection.

Design Option 3: Calculating Kanban Lot Sizes

There is more to performing kanban lot sizes than simply applying a kanban formula. How the kanban lot sizes are calculated depends upon a number of environmental factors, such as the quantity of part numbers that are being calculated, whether there are both kanban and MRP items supporting each other, the number of levels in the bill of materials, the linearity of anticipated demand, and the capability of the manufacturing shop in minimizing lot sizing. Selecting an improper technique in calculating kanban lot sizes for your environment can have serious consequences that come in the form of inflated inventory coupled with shortages and hot lists. Prior to automation and implementation throughout the plant, any technique selected must be thoroughly understood and manually tested on a sample quantity of part numbers to ensure it is correct for your environment. The following sections discuss three diverse environments; these are intended to demonstrate how different kanban techniques are applied in calculating kanban lot sizes to meet the specific needs of the environment. We begin by dealing with the most complex environment and work our way down to the simplest environment. A number of the items discussed will be new to the reader, and appropriate time and effort should be spent to fully understand the logic of the kanban calculation techniques in relationship to the environments presented. At the least, it will be understood that there is no such thing as one size fits all when it comes to applying kanban techniques, because the selection of techniques must be based upon the environmental factors.

Kanban Technique 1: Synchronized Explosion™

An MRP explosion coupled with a simulation routine will handle both MRP items and kanban items.

Environmental Factors for Kanban Technique 1

- The master production schedule contains some degree of lot sizing.
- The bill of materials consists of both single and multilevel.
- MRP items and kanban items are applied to the facility.
- There are hundreds or thousands of part numbers.
- One-piece flow does not exist throughout the whole facility.
- Backflushing with deduct points is applied to the facility.

Application of Kanban Technique 1

This environment is quite common and can be daunting, especially when the practitioner is armed only with an overly simplistic three-part-number example of how to calculate kanban lot sizes. The Synchronized Explosion™ is designed to deal with four major environmental hurdles.

- Hundreds or thousands of part numbers must be recalculated each planning period. This quantity of part numbers is far more than can be dealt with manually and must, therefore, have the kanban lot size calculation process automated.
- The master production schedule contains some degree of lot sizing, which creates nonlinear demand patterns for kanban items that support the final product build, which creates stockouts. The kanban items supporting the master production schedule must be made aware of the nonlinearity during the calculation process to advert stockouts.
- When dealing with multilevel bills of material that contain both MRP items and kanban items, typically we have MRP items going into kanban items, kanban items going into kanban items, and kanban items going into MRP items. Consider, as an example, MRP items or kanban items that support an upper-level kanban item that employs a kanban

container option with a kanban order quantity greater than a one-for-one. For this type of item, you must know when the upper-level kanban will be triggered, and you must know the respective quantity during the kanban lot size calculation process to avoid stockouts.

- You may also have an issue when kanban items that support MRP items are unaware of whether the MRP item is lot sized due to lack of one-piece flow capability. During the kanban lot size calculation process, the kanban item must be made aware of the MRP lot size in the calculation process to avoid stockouts.

The Synchronized Explosion™ is designed to handle the simplest to the most complex environment. It employs a modified MRP program coupled with a simulation routine that is programmed in-house and is demonstrated starting with the construction of the master production schedule, which, in this example, is used to drive final assembly:

- **Master production schedule:** The master production schedule has been load-smoothed to the best ability of the facility. It is created after taking the forecast, customer orders, capacity, and on-hand status into consideration. (See Figure 3-1.) The master production schedule in MRP will not go gross to net because on-hand inventory was already taken into consideration, but it will be offset to provide accurate timing to supporting items.

Final Product	November														
	1	2	5	6	7	8	9	12	13	14	15	16	19	20	21
91 A	130	0	70	65	0	135	0	135	0	100	120	0	100	115	0

Figure 3-1. Lot-sized master production schedule.

- **Bill of material:** The multilevel bill of material for final product number 91A is reflected in Figure 3-2. The MRP will use the bill of material to explode final product 91A requirements. Note that the low-level code is reflected on the right-hand side, which is used by MRP to determine when it has gathered all the gross requirements for a given item. Also note that there are both MRP items and kanban items that make up the bill of material structure.

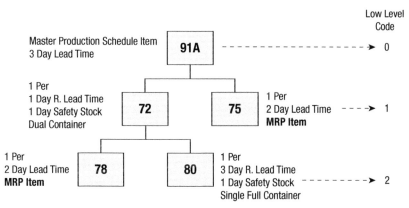

Figure 3-2. Bill of material for final product 91A.

Step 1: MRP Explosion Process: Level 0

The master production schedule interfaces with MRP. (See Figure 3-3.) The explosion process at Level 0 will not go gross to net against the on-hand inventory for Level 0 (Part number 91A). Why? Because in the construction of the master production schedule, finished goods on hand was already taken into consideration. MRP will also not go gross to net based upon an open factory work order. Why? Because factory work orders are not used to pull material from the stockroom to build final product. Instead, materials are located at the point of use, and deduct points and backflushing are used to gradually decrease the on-hand inventory balance as consumption occurs. (*On-hand inventory* is inventory that has not been consumed and remains available for use.) *Note:* Deduct points are intermediate points of completion. They are used to subtract from the on-hand inventory of items that has been applied to the partially completed parent at various positions in the production process and places those part numbers and respective quantities into a limbo inventory account. (*Limbo inventory* is inventory that has been consumed in the manufacturing process, but the parent has not been completed.) At the end of the production line, a backflush will take place, informing the system of the quantity and part number of the parent that was just completed. The backflush will subtract the supporting part numbers and respective quantities that were applied from the on-hand inventory that was consumed from the last deduct point to the backflush point, and will also subtract from the limbo inventory account what was placed there by each deduct point. The backflush will also increment the part number and quantity of what was produced.

The master production schedule MRP explosion will place the gross requirements straight down into the Net Requirements row, and then perform a lead-time offset into the Planned Order Release row based on the lead time (3 days) for part number 91A as shown in Figure 3-3. We can see that 200 pieces will appear in the Planned Order Release row, past due (PD), followed by 65 units for November 1st, and so on. Once MRP is done offsetting Level 0, MRP will multiply the quantity per (noted in the bill of material for part number 75 and 72) times the planned order release quantity in each column, and place the quantities straight down directly into the level 1 Gross Requirements row. See part numbers 75 and 72.

Step 2: MRP Explosion Process: Level 1

Prior to going gross to net at Level 1, the system will determine whether the item is a kanban item or MRP item based on the planner code number or some other attribute that makes the distinction. Once the system makes the distinction, the following will occur for Level 1 items (MRP items at Level 1 are handled first, and then kanban items):

- **MRP items:** MRP will first add the quantity that is in the limbo inventory account to the on-hand inventory that resides at the point of use; in this example, part number 75 has a total on hand of 273 pieces. MRP will be handled as normally and go gross to net and then offset the net requirements into the Planned Order Release column. (See Figure 3-3.) *Note:* The full master production schedule needs to be built, and

Figure 3-3. Level 0 to Level 1 explosion.

91A Final Product — LEVEL 0, Final Product, 3 Day Lead Time

91A Final Product	PD	November 1	2	5	6	7	8	9	12	13	14	15	16	19	20	21
Gross requirements		130	0	70	65	0	135	0	135	0	100	120	0	100	115	0
Scheduled receipts																
Projected on-hand	200															
Net requirements		130	0	70	65	0	135	0	135	0	100	120	0	100	115	0
Planned order release	200	65	0	135	0	135	0	100	120	0	100	115	0			

75 Component — LEVEL 1, MRP Item, 2 Day Lead Time

75 Component	PD	November 1	2	5	6	7	8	9	12	13	14	15	16	19	20	21
Gross requirements	200	65	0	135	0	135	0	100	120	0	100	115	0			
Scheduled receipts																
Projected on-hand	273	73	8	8												
Net requirements				127		135		100	120		100	115				
Planned order release		127		135		100	120		100	115						

72 Assembly — LEVEL 1, Kanban Item, Assembly

72 Assembly	PD	November 1	2	5	6	7	8	9	12	13	14	15	16	19	20	21
Gross requirements	200	65	0	135	0	135	0	100	120	0	100	115	0			
Scheduled receipts																
Projected on-hand	200	0														
Net requirements		65	0	135	0	135	0	100	120	0	100	115	0			
Planned order release	146	146		146		146		146	146		146	146				

← Simulation Results

those MRP supporting items in the limbo inventory account and on-hand inventory are meant to cover the master production schedule.

- **Kanban items:** For kanban items, the only inventory recognized by the MRP for gross to net purposes is the quantity that is in the limbo inventory account. The on-hand inventory quantity residing in the kanban containers is not taken into consideration in MRP gross to net, but rather will be used in the kanban simulation. Why? Look at Figure 3-3, assembly part number 72. There are 200 pieces in the limbo account. This quantity has already been taken from the kanban container(s) and will satisfy 200 pieces of gross requirements, which has not been backflushed as yet. This would leave a need for 65 pieces for November 1st, 0 for November 2nd, 135 pieces for November 5th, and so on. This is the kanban anticipated demand by day that will be used by the simulation going against what is currently in the on-hand inventory quantity residing in the kanban containers. The quantity currently in the containers (on-hand inventory in this example is 70 pieces) is what will be used in the kanban simulation going against the daily demand.

In addition, for kanban items, MRP will not be made aware of any triggered kanban orders (that is, purchased or manufacturing scheduled receipts) because they, too, will be used in the kanban simulation to determine the kanban lot size and precise timing and quantities of what will be triggered. *Note:* Although factory work order numbers are automatically assigned to triggered manufactured items, they are used only as a reference number so that the simulation routine is aware of the specifics of what has been triggered. The factory work orders are not used to pull material from the stockroom, because the material is located at the point of use.

Step 3: Kanban Simulation Level 1

Once MRP has gone gross to net for Level 1 MRP items and offset them into the Planned Order Release row, MRP will then go gross to net on the kanban items, based on what is in limbo inventory, and then freeze the MRP explosion so that the kanban simulation routine can calculate kanban lot sizes and perform a simulation for each kanban item. There is a kanban simulation routine for each container type (single discrete, single full, dual, triple, and multiple) that emulates the mechanics of how each of these container options operate at the point of use. The dual container simulation will be demonstrated for part number 72. (See Figure 3-4.) The information required to perform the simulation has been posted by the system. The simulation for the dual container begins by first determining the quantity that is in each container. This is straightforward, because it is determined by the system knowing the old kanban lot size, which is stored in the MRPII or Enterprise Resource Planning (ERP) system. In this example, the old kanban lot size was 60, and there are currently 70 pieces on hand. By subtracting the old kanban lot size of 60 pieces from the on-hand inventory of 70 pieces, the system has determined that there are 10 pieces in first container (KB1) that are in front, ready for use, and 60 pieces in the container behind it (KB2). The user has set the kanban simulation to pick up 10 manufacturing days of projected MRP net requirements (November 1 to November 14, 2007). It will first add up the net requirement demand, which equals 655 pieces, and then divide by the number of manufacturing days it went out in time, which was 10 days, to equal an average daily demand of 66 pieces, rounded up. The average daily demand of 66 pieces is then multiplied by the total of 1-day replenishment lead time and 1-day of safety stock (66-piece average daily demand) × (1-day replenishment lead time + 1-day safety stock) to equal a preliminary kanban lot size of 132 pieces. If minimums and multiples are to be applied, they would be applied at this point in time. In this example, however, minimums and multiples do not apply. The kanban simulation routine will then extract from the computer system the due date and on-order quantity of triggered containers and place it at the appropriate date in the simulation Download on Order Due column.

In this example, there are no triggered kanban orders. The kanban simulation routine begins to test the preliminary kanban lot size

Kanban Simulation

Part Number: 72
Description: Left Holder
Parts Grid Row Number: 2
Item Container Option: 3-Dual
Start KB1: 10   Start KB2: 60

Old Kanban Lot Size: 60
On Hand Quantity: 70
Average Daily Demand: 66
Replenishment Lead: 1

Safety Stock: 1
MDays: 10

Date	Demand	KB1 Ending	KB2 Ending	Download On Order due	Trigger Due	Total Received	Simulated Trigger	Total Simulated Orders Outstanding	Ending On Hand
Simulation Try Number: 1				**Preliminary Kanban Lot Size: 132**					
1 11/1/07	65	0	5	0	0	0	132	132	5
2 11/2/07	0	132	5	0	132	132	0	0	137
3 11/5/07	135	2	0	0	0	0	132	132	2
4 11/6/07	0	2	132	0	132	132	0	0	134
5 11/7/07	135	0	0	0	0	0	264	264	-1

Stockout on day 5 with lead time days of 1. Lot size failed on day 5 (shortage of 1), will raise lot size and try again.

Date	Demand	KB1 Ending	KB2 Ending	Download On Order due	Trigger Due	Total Received	Simulated Trigger	Total Simulated Orders Outstanding	Ending On Hand
Simulation Try Number: 2				**Preliminary Kanban Lot Size: 146**					
1 11/1/07	65	0	5	0	0	0	146	146	5
2 11/2/07	0	146	5	0	146	146	0	0	151
3 11/5/07	135	16	0	0	0	0	146	146	16
4 11/6/07	0	16	146	0	146	146	0	0	162
5 11/7/07	135	0	27	0	0	0	146	146	27
6 11/8/07	0	146	27	0	146	146	0	0	173
7 11/9/07	100	73	0	0	0	0	146	146	73
8 11/12/07	120	0	99	0	146	146	146	146	99
9 11/13/07	0	146	99	0	146	146	146	0	245
10 11/14/07	100	145	0	0	0	0	146	146	145

Highest on hand stock level 245 observed on MDay 9. Lowest on hand stock level 5 observed on MDay 1. Average on hand stock level 109. Final lot size 146.

Figure 3-4. Simulation for part number 72.

of 132 pieces by first applying KB1 container, which has 10 pieces in it, against MRP demand of 65 on November 1, 2007, leaving an unsatisfied quantity of 55 pieces. The simulation routine at this point in time will simulate a trigger for the KB1 empty container under the column called Simulated Trigger for 132 pieces, which is the preliminary kanban lot size being tested (dual containers are triggered when empty). The simulation will then consume the unsatisfied demand of 55 pieces from KB2, leaving 5 pieces in KB2. On November 2, 2007, there is zero demand. However, according to the lead time of 1 day, KB1 has received the 132 pieces that were triggered the day before (see Total Received column). On November 5, 2007, there is an MRP demand for 135 pieces. The 5 pieces remaining in KB2 are applied, thus emptying and triggering KB2 for 132 pieces, as shown under the Simulated Triggered column. KB1 moves forward, and 130 pieces are applied from it, satisfying the requirement and leaving 2 pieces in the container. On November 6, 2007, there is no MRP demand; however, 132 pieces that were triggered the day before for KB2 have been received. Finally, on November 7, 2007, both KB1 and KB2 stock out as they try to satisfy a 135-piece requirement, leaving an unsatisfied demand of 1 piece (see the column called Ending On Hand). A *stockout* is defined as having an unsatisfied demand with zero on hand. The simulation routine will stop and determine whether elevating the preliminary kanban lot size will avert the stockout. If the stockout occurs beyond the replenishment lead time, elevating the preliminary kanban lot size would avert the stockout. If the stockout occurred within replenishment lead time (e.g., November 1, 2007), elevating the preliminary kanban lot size would not help because it is dealing with a timing issue. Because the stockout occurred beyond replenishment lead time, the simulation will elevate the preliminary kanban lot size by the user simulation setting, which in this case is 10 percent. Therefore, the original preliminary kanban lot size will be elevated to $(1.10) \times (132) = 146$ pieces rounded. The simulation will begin again under the heading Simulation Try Number 2. This time, the simulation has not encountered a stockout and 146 pieces have now been accepted as the final kanban lot size.

Step 4: Post kanban simulation results to MRP Planned Order Release column

Because this kanban item part number 72 passed, the kanban simulation routine will now pick up from the Simulated Trigger column (under Simulation Try Number 2) the timing and quantities of what will be triggered, by when (e.g., 146 11/1/2007, 146 11/5/2007, and so on), and place them in MRP's Planned Order Release row for part number 72, as shown in Figure 3-5. The parts that go into part number 72 will now be alerted as to the quantity and date the trigger will occur to ensure they are available. The supporting parts sets must be made available on the day the trigger will occur, because production can commence on the day of the trigger.

The system will then add up the triggered orders that existed and were placed in simulation in the Downloaded On Order Due column if they exist, and place the total quantity in the first time period (e.g., November 1, 2007) of the MRP's Planned Order Release row. Why? These already triggered orders are requirements that need to be supported by the lower level and were counted on in the simulation to cover demand if they exist. They are not placed in MRP based on the trigger order due date, because the material needs to be available the day it is triggered. In this example, for part number 72, there were no triggered orders prior to the simulation.

Step 5: MRP Released to Explode to Level 2

Once all the MRP item and kanban item calculations and simulations have taken place for Level 1, Level 1 Planned Order Release items are handed straight down to the Level 2 items Gross Requirements row after the quantity per has been multiplied, as reflected in Figure 3-5.

Step 6: Level 2 Calculations

The same process covered in Level 1 is repeated. MRP item 78 in Figure 3-5 simply goes gross to net and offsets. Kanban component number 80 goes gross to net in MRP, using the quantity of inventory in the limbo account, and MRP is then frozen for Level 2.

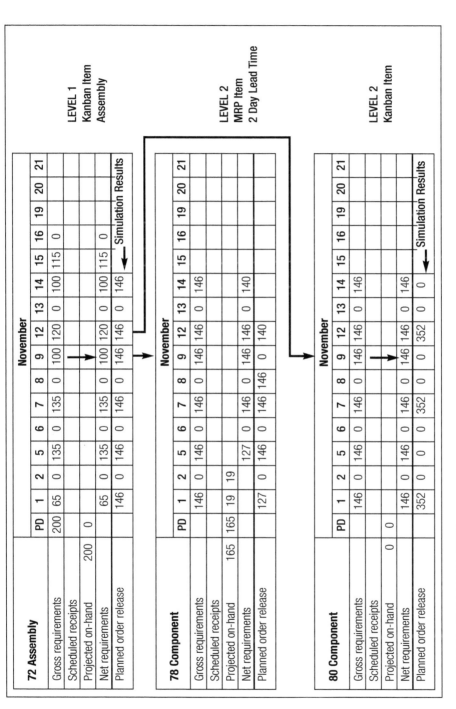

Figure 3-5. Level 1 to Level 2 explosion.

In this example, there was zero inventory in the limbo account. The MRP net requirements and required fields are placed in the kanban simulation routine to calculate a preliminary kanban lot size and test it to ensure that nonlinear demand patterns do not generate a stockout, as reflected in Figure 3-6. Because part number 80 is a single container full option, it has a different simulation routine that emulates the mechanics of triggering for this container option. When the total of on-hand and triggered on-order inventory falls below the calculated kanban lot size, a trigger occurs (see Figure 3-6). As you can see, the on-hand inventory of 365 pieces is applied to the demand of 146 pieces for November 1, 2007, leaving 219 pieces in KB1 (only 1 container). Because it fell below the preliminary kanban lot size of 352 pieces and there are no triggered orders, a kanban is triggered for the full kanban lot size of 352 pieces, as reflected in the Simulated Trigger column. On November 2, 2007, there is no demand, and we now move to November 5, 2007, where the remaining 219 pieces that are on hand are applied to the 146 MRP demand, leaving 73 pieces in the container. On November 6, 2007, there is no demand; however, based on the replenishment lead time of 3 days, the simulated trigger for 352 pieces that occurred on November 1, 2007 has been received as reflected in the Total Received column, elevating the on hand inventory in KB1 to 425 pieces. This continues all the way down in the same manner through Day 10.

Because part number 80 has passed the simulation, the preliminary kanban lot size of 352 pieces now becomes the final kanban lot size, and the simulated trigger quantity by their respective time periods are posted to MRP's Planned Order Release row, as reflected in Figure 3-5.

In addition, the system will then add up the download on order due quantities if they exist, and place the total quantity in the first time period (e.g., November 1, 2007) of the MRP's Planned Order Release row. Why? These triggered orders are requirements that need to be supported by the lower level and were counted on in the simulation to cover demand. In this example, for part number 80, there were no triggered orders prior to the simulation.

Kanban Simulation

Part Number: 80
Description: Order Lever
Parts Grid Row Number: 3
Item Container Option: 2-Single Full
Start KB1: 365

On Hand Quantity: 365
Average Daily Demand: 88
Replenishment Lead: 3

Safety Stock: 1
MDays: 10

Simulation Try Number: 1

Preliminary Kanban Lot Size: 352

	Date	Demand	KB1 Ending	KB2 Ending	Download On Order due	Trigger Due	Total Received	Simulated Trigger	Total Simulated Orders Outstanding	Ending On Hand
1	11/1/07	146	219	N/A	0	0	0	352	352	219
2	11/2/07	0	219	N/A	0	0	0	0	352	219
3	11/5/07	146	73	N/A	0	0	0	0	352	73
4	11/6/07	0	425	N/A	0	352	352	0	0	425
5	11/7/07	146	279	N/A	0	0	0	352	352	279
6	11/8/07	0	279	N/A	0	0	0	0	352	279
7	11/9/07	146	133	N/A	0	0	0	0	352	133
8	11/12/07	146	339	N/A	0	352	352	352	352	339
9	11/13/07	0	339	N/A	0	0	0	0	352	339
10	11/14/07	146	193	N/A	0	0	0	0	352	193

Highest on hand stock level 425 observed on MDay 4. Lowest on hand stock level 73 observed on MDay 3. Average on hand stock level 249. Final lot size 352.

Figure 3-6. Single container full simulation part number 80.

45

Because all Level 2 items have been calculated, MRP would be released to continue this process level by level until there were no more levels remaining in the bills of material. See Appendix B to learn how single discrete and multiple containers are simulated (under the heading of Simulation).

Step 7: If the Simulation Fails Within Lead Time

If any of the kanban container options fail within lead time during simulation, the simulation will stop and will accept the preliminary kanban lot size as the final kanban lot size and generate an exception report for user intervention. (See Appendix B.)

In addition, based on the specific container option, the following will occur for failed simulation items:

- **Single container discrete:** The MRP net requirements will be placed in MRP's Planned Order Release row after it has been offset by the replenishment lead time.
- **Multiple container:** The MRP Net requirements will be placed in MRP's planned order release after it has been lot sized by the standard container quantity and offset by the replenishment lead time.
- **Single Full, Dual, and Triple:** The MRP net requirements will be placed in MRP's Planned Order Release row after it has been lot sized by the preliminary kanban lot size that failed the simulation and then offset by the replenishment lead time.

Note 1: We have not pared down the net requirements by the on-hand inventory in the kanban containers. Why? The reason for a stockout within lead time is typically due to a spike in demand (a single large requirement that is within replenishment lead time). This approach is optional, but typically it is best not to minimize the degree of supporting part numbers inventory being planned until we can look at the exception reports and determine the issue. This is investigated immediately after the explosion/simulation process employing the exception reports.

Note 2: Already triggered on orders (download on order due) will not be added to MRP's Planned Order Release row for failed simulated items. Why? Because the full demand is already carried in MRP's net requirements. Bear in mind that when we simulate, the simulation takes into consideration the net requirements, what is on hand in the containers, and what has already been triggered (downloaded on order due). From this information, the simulation is saying these additional orders will be triggered by this point in time and placed into the MRP Planned Order Release column. Then, we must add back into the Planned Order Release column the items that were triggered, because they need supporting parts or material if they are manufactured items. Because the full weight of the demand is in the net requirements, which has not passed the simulation, this will suffice until we immediately investigate, using the exception reports.

Note 3: For failed simulation items, you will lot size the net requirements by the failed preliminary kanban lot size and offset. Why? Because the lot size is the closest thing that you have to what the triggered quantity would be. You perform an offset to represent the closest thing you have to when the supporting material may be required from a triggering standpoint. This is intended to satisfy the completion of the MRP explosion, which at its conclusion will generate an exception report on the part numbers that failed the simulation for immediate user intervention.

The Synchronized Explosion™ can be applied to most ERP/MRPII packages and in most cases achieved without changing source code. This is typically accomplished by securing a copy of the existing MRP module. This copy is modified to freeze the MRP explosion at each level (low level code), apply the simulation routine on kanban items, and accept the kanban simulation routines' simulated trigger information in the MRP's Planned Order Release row, along with any other already triggered kanban orders. The kanban simulation routine is programmed in-house to calculate kanban lot sizes, perform the simulation, hand the simulated trigger results to MRP, and generate the necessary exception reports for failed simulated items for user intervention.

Note: Before modifying anything, it is key to read the balance of this book to identify all automated features that may be required and to follow in detail the prescribed implementation methodologies that pertain to this or any other technique discussed. In short, this and all other techniques must first be applied manually to the environment, with sample part numbers, to prove without question that the techniques selected will work for your environment. Your IT person or group will determine the best approach for your particular ERP/MRPII package where automation is required.

The majority of the computer fields exist in most ERP/MRPII packages to accommodate the preceding approach. An additional 7 to 9 fields may need to be added in most cases to fully automate the calculation, triggering, and the many other automated kanban techniques covered in this book. It will take between 20 and 25 person-days to program the MRP enhancements and simulation routines. When comparing the cost and time of putting this technique in place to the direct and indirect costs associated with even one month's worth of stockouts, high inventory levels, missed customer shipments, expedites, and excessive staff to operate an ineffective system, it makes good business sense to address the issue rather than try to live with it.

Key Notes

1. The kanban simulation requires that the lead times be expressed in whole-day increments.
2. If kanban is going to drive the final assembly build, the level 0 MRP explosion for the product master production schedule will have to be simulated to calculate the kanban lot size and reflect the timing and quantities of the trigger.
3. Projected net requirements that are picked up to calculate kanban lot sizes must go out far enough in time to calculate kanban lot sizes. This must equal a distance of two times the longest kanban replenishment lead time, plus the explosion frequency. (See Appendix B.)
4. Selecting kanban candidates is very important and is covered in Chapter 8. Placing highly erratic items on kanban inflates inventory, degrades the triggering process, and creates a number of situations requiring user intervention.

5. *The Synchronized Explosion™ emulates kanban exactly as if it were at the point of use. The advantage is that it will adjust kanban lot sizes automatically to avert shortages due to nonlinear demand. It also provides the exact timing and quantities of what will be triggered, by what date, and relays that information directly to MRP items and kanban items that support its production. The Synchronized Explosion™ also raises the flag if a stockout cannot be averted by elevating the kanban lot size. This permits user intervention prior to the stockout.*

Kanban Technique 2: Spreadsheet Calculations

The load-smooth master production schedule is interfaced with MRP, which is exploded. The gross requirements for kanban items are picked up and placed in a spreadsheet program, where the average daily demand is calculated and applied to the kanban lot size formula.

Environmental Factors for Kanban Technique 2

- Every item in the master production schedule is load-smoothed.
- There is a single-level bill of material. There are no multi-level bills of material.
- MRP items and kanban items are applied to the facility.
- Backflushing with deduct points is applied to the facility.

Application of Kanban Technique 2

The load-smooth master production schedule is used to drive the final product build and, when interfaced with MRP (Level 0), does not go gross to net against on-hand inventory but will offset based on lead time. On-hand inventory was already taken into consideration in the construction of the load-smooth master production schedule and represents what is to be built. MRP will continue its explosion to the supporting level (Level 1), go gross to net based against on-hand and on-order inventory, and offset according to the replenishment lead time. In other words, MRP is oblivious if an item is an MRP item or kanban item and will be handled as usual. For kanban items, the user will program a routine to create an ASCII flat file by extracting data from the MRP explosion and database. This flat file will include the kanban part number, description, replenishment lead time, safety-stock setting, minimums, multiples, and daily MRP gross requirements starting with day 1 and going out in distance according to the user's setting. The ASCII flat file is then interfaced with a simple spreadsheet, which will acquire the file, add up the gross requirements, divide the total gross requirements by the number of manufacturing days it had to go out in time to gather the gross requirements, calculate the average daily demand, and apply it to the kanban lot size formula.

Here is an example: The load-smooth master production schedule is constructed. (See Figure 3-7.) It contains two master schedule items, part numbers 51A and 51B. The master production schedule bill of materials is reflected in Figure 3-8. The master production

Final Product	November										
	1	2	5	6	7	8	9	12	13	14	15
51 A	240	240	240	240	240	240	240	240	240	240	240
51 B	120	120	120	120	120	120	120	120	120	120	120

Figure 3-7. Load-smooth master production schedule.

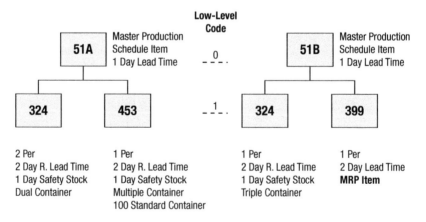

Figure 3-8. Master production schedule bill of materials.

schedule is interfaced with MRP, and the master production schedule item does not go gross to net based on on-hand inventory. It will offset per the replenishment lead time. (See Figure 3-9.) The MRP will explode out the bill of materials (see Figure 3-10), going gross to net based on on-hand inventory and scheduled receipts, and will offset according to replenishment lead time. On completion of MRP's explosion, an ASCII flat file is created that picks up the prescribed information and is interfaced with the spreadsheet calculation program, which then calculates the kanban lot sizes. The user setting for gathering the gross requirements was 10 manufacturing days. (See Figure 3-11.)

Key Notes

1. *The program will not start picking up gross requirements from the past due for Level 1 kanban items to place in the spreadsheet. The reason we permit the offsetting is to keep MRP items accurate at Level 1, as it requires the lead-time offset. Because the gross demand is perfectly linear, this is technically correct for kanban items.*

2. *Projected gross requirements that are picked up to calculate kanban lot sizes must go out far enough in time to calculate kanban lot sizes. This must equal a distance of twice the longest kanban replenishment lead time, plus explosion frequency. (See Appendix B.)*

3. *Because the demand is perfectly linear, and because demand does not have lower-level supporting items that need to know when kanban will be triggered and for what quantities, we do not need to simulate.*

4. *This technique can be performed manually if you are dealing with only a handful of part numbers.*

5. *If kanban is going to be driving the final assembly build versus being driven by a master production schedule, kanban technique 2 should not be applied, because the level 1 kanban and MRP items need to be aware of the precise timing and quantity of the upper-level trigger. In this case, kanban technique 1 should be considered for application.*

"51 A" Final Product
1 Day Lead Time

	PD	November										
		1	2	5	6	7	8	9	12	13	14	15
Gross requirements		240	240	240	240	240	240	240	240	240	240	240
Scheduled Receipts												
Projected on-hand												
Net requirements		240	240	240	240	240	240	240	240	240	240	240
Planned order release	240	240	240	240	240	240	240	240	240	240	240	240

"51 B" Final Product
1 Day Lead Time

	PD	November										
		1	2	5	6	7	8	9	12	13	14	15
Gross requirements		120	120	120	120	120	120	120	240	120	120	120
Scheduled Receipts												
Projected on-hand												
Net requirements		120	120	120	120	120	120	120	120	120	120	120
Planned order release	120	120	120	120	120	120	120	120	120	120	120	120

Figure 3-9. Master schedule MRP explosion: Level 0.

324 Part Number
2 Day R. Lead Time
Kanban Item — 1,300

	PD	\(\leftarrow\) November \(\rightarrow\)										
	PD	1	2	5	6	7	8	9	12	13	14	15
Gross requirements	600	600	600	600	600	600	600	600	600	600	600	600
Scheduled Receipts												
Projected on-hand	700	100										
Net requirements			500	600	600	600	600	600	600	600	600	600
Planned order release	500	600	600	600	600	600	600	600	600	600	600	600

453 Part Number
2 Day R. Lead Time
Kanban Item — 555

	PD	\(\leftarrow\) November \(\rightarrow\)										
	PD	1	2	5	6	7	8	9	12	13	14	15
Gross requirements	240	240	240	240	240	240	240	240	240	240	240	240
Scheduled Receipts												
Projected on-hand	315	75										
Net requirements			165	240	240	240	240	240	240	240	240	240
Planned order release	165	240	240	240	240	240	240	240	240	240	240	240

399 Part Number
2 Day Lead Time
MRP Item — 550

	PD	\(\leftarrow\) November \(\rightarrow\)										
	PD	1	2	5	6	7	8	9	12	13	14	15
Gross requirements	120	120	120	120	120	120	120	120	120	120	120	120
Scheduled Receipts												
Projected on-hand	430	310	190	70								
Net requirements					50	120	120	120	120	120	120	120
Planned order release			50	120	120	120	120	120	120	120	120	120

Figure 3-10. MRP Explosion: Level 1

Part Number	R. Lead Time	Safety Stock	Min.	Mul.	Nov 1	Nov 2	Nov 5	Nov 6	Nov 7
324	2	1			600	600	600	600	600
453	2	1		100	240	240	240	240	240

Nov 8	Nov 9	Nov 12	Nov 13	Nov 14	Total	A.D.D.	Kanban Lot Size	Number Containers
600	600	600	600	600	6,000	600	1,800	
240	240	240	240	240	2,400	240	800	8

Figure 3-11. Spreadsheet kanban lot size calculations.

Kanban Technique 3: Historical Usage Kanban Calculation Routine

Acquire, adjust, and apply historical usage data to calculate kanban lot sizes.

Environmental Factors for Kanban Technique 3

- The facility is a job shop.
- Specific finished goods demand cannot be forecasted. Shipment dollars are forecasted.
- There is a high degree of commonality at the lower levels.
- There are hundreds or thousands of kanban candidates.

Application of Kanban Technique 3

Have the computer programmed to perform the following steps:

- **Step 1:** The user will input into the kanban calculation routine a "from" date and a "to" date and a times factor into the kanban calculation program. The *from date* tells the system when to begin picking up historical usage quantities by part number for kanban items. The *to date* represents the last point in time the program will pick up historical usage. The *times factor* tells the routine how much to increase or decrease the historical quantities that were picked up based

on current dollar forecasts as compared to historical shipment dollars that occurred between the *from date* and *to
date*. For example, today is November 1, 2007. We will set
the *from* date at 10/01/2007 and the *to* date at 10/31/2007.
This represents 23 manufacturing days. Last month, we
shipped out $6 million in product, and this month we
expect to ship out $6.6 million. We will, therefore, set our
times factor at 1.1 ($6.6 million/$6 million).

- **Step 2:** The routine will then gather the historical usage
quantities for each kanban item from the database that have
a unique identifier (planner code or some other attribute)
and then multiply the historical usage quantity times the
times factor. The adjusted historical usage quantity for each
kanban item will then be divided by the number of manufacturing days it had to go back into the past to determine
the average daily demand. The routine will then apply the
average daily demand to the kanban lot size formula.

For example, the historical demand for part number 453 that
was picked up equaled 2,300 pieces. It was then multiplied by the
1.1 times factor which elevated it to 2,530 pieces. This number was
then divided by the 23 manufacturing days to equal an average
daily demand of 110 pieces. Part number 453 is a multiple container option and has a replenishment lead time of 4 days, safety
stock of 1 day, and a standard container quantity of 50 pieces. The
calculated kanban lot size would be calculated to equal (110-piece
average daily demand) × (4-day replenishment lead time + 1-day
safety stock) = 550 pieces, which equates to (550 piece kanban lot
size/50 standard container quantity) 11 containers, rounded up per
the multiple.

Key Notes

1. *What occurs if the supporting item below the kanban item is a kanban
item? Its historical demand will be picked up and have its kanban lot size
calculated. Why don't we care about the timing of triggering and quantity
triggered for the kanban items discussed in this chapter? The issue is that*

we do not have a master production schedule with quantities and dates. What we do have is historical data adjusted by a times factor. What is important is not to have an upper-level kanban item employing a full kanban lot size container option, with a lower-level kanban item employing a single container discrete.

2. *Job shops typically carry commonly used raw materials, which significantly improves their customer response time. This is typically what gets placed on kanban in these environments.*

3. *Determining kanban candidates and required levels of safety stock to avert stockouts is covered in Chapter 8. This kanban design option must be applied if this calculation methodology is being employed.*

Conclusion

Ideally, bills of material should be flattened, lean manufacturing should be fully put into place (enabling a one-piece flow), and the top-level build should be completely linear permitting a simple application of a kanban formula when dealing with a handful of part numbers. Unfortunately, this is not the typical profile of most companies, and just simply applying a kanban formula to a nonlinear demand pattern item is a recipe for stockout. Trying to compensate for nonlinear demand patterns by applying a large degree of safety stock will degrade the triggering process and inflate inventory. Part of the solution was first discussed in Chapter 2: load-smoothing the master production schedule as much as possible. This, combined with implementing lean to the fullest extent possible, is an appropriate measure. However, there is no escaping the reality of having to identify the current environmental factors and selecting the appropriate kanban techniques when implementing kanban. Companies with less-than-perfect demand patterns can achieve significant levels of success in reducing their current inventory levels, shortages, obsolescence, and operating cost. In order to achieve these results, companies must be aware of their specific environmental factors and design a kanban system that is tailored to fit the needs of their environment.

In Chapter 4, we cover kanban containers and triggering.

KANBAN CONTAINER, TRIGGERING, AND MAINTENANCE

S electing the appropriate kanban container option is critical, because each container option is designed to serve a specific environmental need. Some kanban container options are designed to trigger only what has been consumed (highly expensive items not constrained by setup time issues), while others launch full kanban lot sizes (to minimize transportation cost for inexpensive purchased items). If you were dealing with only a handful of part numbers in a relatively small manufacturing environment, manual triggering would be applicable, because it can be managed relatively quickly and effectively. However, if you're dealing with thousands of part numbers, the automation of triggering is mandatory because it enables many other required automation tools to be leveraged by having the triggered information in the computer. Maintenance is all important, because the recalculation of kanban necessitates speed and diligence in providing current and accurate information. The objective of these tools is to initiate specific action in a specific manner tailored to meet the specific needs of the environment. Within this kanban design category are five kanban design options that work together to control the lean environment. The five kanban design options are as follows:

- Design Option 4: Kanban Container Options
- Design Option 5: Multiple Kanban Card Option
- Design Option 6: Triggering
- Design Option 7: Alternative Triggering Methods
- Design Option 8: System Maintenance

This chapter discusses the individual design options and their respective techniques.

Design Option 4: Kanban Container Options

You have five basic container options from which to choose. These are single discrete, single full, dual, triple, and multiple. It is not unusual to find more than one container option employed within a given environment. In fact, most companies find it necessary to apply a variety of container options, each of which is selected based on specific environmental conditions. This includes such factors as demand volume, size, weight, cost of the item, distance of supplier, transportation cost, setup time, and inventory accuracy.

Kanban Technique 1: Single Discrete Container

The single discrete container is typically computerized and automatically triggered when the total of on-hand and on-order goods falls below the kanban lot size.

Environmental Factors for Kanban Technique 1

- These are highly expensive items.
- Setup time is not an issue.
- The item is too large for a container.
- Computerized inventory and on-order condition are employed and are accurate.

Application of Kanban Technique 1

This container option is used internally and externally to the plant. When triggered, there is no container that goes back and forth. In application, there may not even be a physical container involved but rather a location where the material is stored, such as at the point of use. The lack of container often is due to the large size of the components. When the total of on-hand and on-order items falls below the calculated kanban lot size, a trigger occurs for the difference. For example, if the kanban lot size is 30 pieces and there are 30 pieces on hand with zero on order, nothing will occur. If 5 pieces are taken, leaving 25 pieces in the container with zero on order, a trigger for 5 pieces will occur. If 2 more pieces are taken, the 23 pieces remaining on hand will be added to the 5 pieces that are on order, equaling a total of 28 pieces. Those pieces are then subtracted from the kanban lot size of 30 pieces (30 piece kanban lot size—a total of 28 pieces on-hand plus on-order inventory), leaving a difference of 2 pieces, which will be triggered.

This container option is typically applied internally to highly expensive items, such as finished goods stock being on kanban, assemblies, and subassemblies, or to the production floor at the point of use for extremely large components. It is also applied to extremely expensive purchased components. This container option carries far less *average inventory* than any of the other container options. Comparing Figure 4-1 to Figure 4-2 clearly demonstrates this point. Both figures have the same lead time, safety stock, demand quantities, and kanban lot size. The only difference is that Figure 4-1 is a single full container and Figure 4-2 is a single discrete container. These kanban simulation models on the right-hand side reflect each day's ending inventory and, at the bottom of the simulation, the average inventory carried is calculated. The kanban lot size for both of these figures is 352 pieces.

The single container full average inventory is 249 pieces, and the single discrete container is 122 pieces average inventory. This is more than a 50 percent difference in the degree of inventory carried. This is what makes the single discrete container a powerful selection when targeting inventory reduction. There are two drawbacks to the application of the single discrete container: The first is that it is lot-size sensitive to what it is supporting. What this means is that if the upper-level item it is supporting has, for example, a kanban lot of 352 pieces and is a dual container (full kanban lot size when triggered) due to its lead time and safety-stock setting, and this single discrete container option kanban lot size is 352 pieces carrying an average of 122 pieces of inventory, a stockout can easily occur. When full kanban lot size items trigger, the supporting material needs to be immediately available. The best application for the single discrete container option is finished goods inventory, assemblies, and subassemblies.

Kanban Simulation

Part Number: 80
Description: Cinder Lever
Parts Grid Row Number: 3
Item Container Option: 2-Single Full
Start KB1: 365

On Hand Quantity: 365
Average Daily Demand: 88
Replenishment Lead: 3

Safety Stock: 1
MDays: 10

Simulation Try Number: 1

Preliminary Kanban Lot Size: 352

	Date	Demand	KB1 Ending	KB2 Ending	Download On Order due	Trigger Due	Total Received	Simulated Trigger	Total Simulated Orders Outstanding	Ending On Hand
1	11/1/07	146	219	N/A	0	0	0	352	352	219
2	11/2/07	0	219	N/A	0	0	0	0	352	219
3	11/5/07	146	73	N/A	0	0	0	0	352	73
4	11/6/07	0	425	N/A	0	352	352	0	0	425
5	11/7/07	146	279	N/A	0	0	0	352	352	279
6	11/8/07	0	279	N/A	0	0	0	0	352	279
7	11/9/07	146	133	N/A	0	0	0	0	352	133
8	11/12/07	146	339	N/A	0	352	352	352	352	339
9	11/13/07	0	339	N/A	0	0	0	0	352	339
10	11/14/07	146	193	N/A	0	0	0	0	352	193

Highest on hand stock level 425 observed on MDay 4. Lowest on hand stock level 73 observed on MDay 3. Average on hand stock level 249. Final lot size 352.

Figure 4-1. Single full container.

Kanban Simulation

Part Number: 80
Description: Cinder Lever
Parts Grid Row Number: 3
Item Container Option: 1-Single Discrete
Start KB1: 365

On Hand Quantity: 365
Average Daily Demand: 88
Replenishment Lead: 3

Safety Stock: 1
MDays: 10

	Date	Demand	KB1 Ending	KB2 Ending	Download On Order due	Trigger Due	Total Received	Simulated Trigger	Total Simulated Orders Outstanding	Ending On Hand
Simulation Try Number: 1										
				Preliminary Kanban Lot Size: 352						
1	11/1/07	146	219	N/A	0	0	0	133	133	219
2	11/2/07	0	219	N/A	0	0	0	0	133	219
3	11/5/07	146	73	N/A	0	0	0	146	279	73
4	11/6/07	0	206	N/A	0	133	133	0	146	206
5	11/7/07	146	60	N/A	0	0	0	146	292	60
6	11/8/07	0	206	N/A	0	146	146	0	146	206
7	11/9/07	146	60	N/A	0	0	0	146	292	60
8	11/12/07	146	60	N/A	0	146	146	146	292	60
9	11/13/07	0	60	N/A	0	0	0	0	292	60
10	11/14/07	146	60	N/A	0	146	146	146	292	60

Highest on hand stock level 219 observed on MDay 1. Lowest on hand stock level 60 observed on MDay 5. Average on hand stock level 122. Final lot size 352.

Figure 4-2. Single discrete container.

The second drawback is that the single discrete container application is best served when applying automated triggering, because the total of on-hand and on-order inventory must be checked frequently against the kanban lot size, which is best administered by the computer system. When applying this container option, the inventory and on-order condition must be accurate. It, however, can be applied successfully with manual triggering, if you're dealing with extremely large items where individual kanban cards are attached to each item. In this case, once consumption occurs, the card is triggered, which represents a quantity of 1. When the item is received, a purchasing *traveler* can automatically be generated for kanban items, reflecting its destination, as shown in Figure 4-3. See the routing instruction on the traveler. If a manual approach is used for the receipt process, a destination list is provided, reflecting the point-of-use location.

Purchasing Traveler

Part number	39114	Supplier	JC Mill
Description	Grip Mount	PO number	Q1435234
Quantity received	100	Quantity ordered	1,350
Date received	11/05/2007	Due date	11/05/2007
Revision	D		

Routing Instruction

No inspection. Floor location Dept 9/Line 3/3C

Quality Notes:

Figure 4-3. Purchasing traveler.

The single discrete container option produces many orders and therefore many receipts. Care must be exercised to minimize its application primarily to finished goods inventory, assemblies, and subassemblies and to extremely large items where floor space is a concern.

Kanban Technique 2: Single Full Container

The single full container is typically computerized and automatically triggered when the total of on-hand and on-order inventory falls below the kanban lot size.

Environmental Factors for Kanban Technique 2

- Items are inexpensive.
- The supplier is at a great distance from the plant.
- Transportation cost of containers is a concern as compared to the cost of the component.
- Components are typically small.
- Internal setup time is an issue, requiring a full kanban lot-size ordering quantity.
- Computerized inventory and on-order condition must be accurate.

Application of Kanban Technique 2

This container option can be applied internally or externally to the plant. When triggered, no container goes back and forth. When the total of on-hand and on-order inventory falls below the calculated kanban lot size, a trigger will occur for the full kanban lot size. For example, if the kanban lot size is 30 pieces and 2 pieces are consumed with zero on-order, a quantity of 30 will be triggered for replenishment. This container option permanently remains at the point of use and does not move when triggered. Typically, there is a container at the point of use to house the item or a location on the production line at the point of use.

This container option is usually applied to inexpensive items when the supplier is at a great distance from the plant. The reason this container option would be chosen is that the return cost of the empty container is too expensive relative to the cost of the part. When the item is received, a purchasing traveler is generated or a destination list is provided reflecting the point of use. When considering this container option for purchased items, bear in mind that the components are typically shipped in a cardboard box and delivered to the production floor, which bring debris into the manufacturing environment. In other words, your production process must not be sensitive to the contaminants. Automated triggering should be applied to this container option, because it would be unrealistic to count the on-hand quantity in the container daily and add it to the on-order quantity, and then compare it to the kanban lot size to determine whether it should be triggered. Computerized inventory and on-order condition must be accurate.

Kanban Technique 3: Dual Containers

The dual container is a good, simple, all-around container option and is a basic mainstay from an application standpoint.

Environmental Factors for Kanban Technique 3

- Small components, which fluctuate in kanban lot sizes from one planning period to the next, can be realistically accommodated in a permanently assigned container.
- Supplier is located within two days of the plant.
- Internal setup time is an issue, requiring a full kanban lot-size ordering quantity.

Application of Kanban Technique 3

The dual container option is used internally and externally to the plant. There are two identical containers, one behind the other. When the front container is emptied, it is triggered for the full kanban lot size. The container that was behind it moves forward for continued use. The empty container goes to the cell or supplier, who is responsible for replenishment. Once filled with the appropriate kanban lot size, the container is returned to the point of use. These containers, when sized for selection for a given part number, are thoroughly researched to understand the variations of the kanban lot size that may exist over an extended period of time. This is to ensure that the selected container can accommodate the quantity differences, given that kanban lot sizes fluctuate from one planning period to the next.

This container option is applied to those items whose supplier is within two days distance from the plant. The main reason this container option would be chosen is that the components are small, the components are not exceedingly expensive, and the container can handle the fluctuation of kanban lot sizes. This container option is also used internally and applied where setup times are an issue, requiring a full kanban lot size to be run. This is a good overall container option, especially where perpetuating accurate inventory is an issue. When the container is emptied, it is simply triggered without reliance on frequent observation, accurate inventory, or accuracy of on-order conditions.

Kanban Technique 4: Triple Containers

The triple container is only used externally to the plant and significantly reduces the overall replenishment lead time.

Environmental Factors for Kanban Technique 4

* Small components, which fluctuate in kanban lot sizes, can be realistically accommodated in a permanently assigned container.
* Supplier is located more than two days from the plant.

Application of Kanban Technique 4

This container option is applied only externally to the supplier. When triggered, the full kanban lot size is ordered. There are two identical containers, one behind the other at the point of use. The third container is identical to the other two and resides empty at the supplier responsible for replenishment. When the front container is emptied, it is triggered for the full kanban lot size. The container that was behind it moves forward for continued use. A triggered signal (for example, phone call, fax, electronic data interchange [EDI], extranet, FTP server) is given to the supplier responsible, who immediately fills the triggered quantity in the empty container and ships it to the manufacturer. Meanwhile, the manufacturer ships the empty kanban container back to the supplier, where it will remain until a container is triggered again. Once the manufacturer receives the replenishment, it will be placed at the point of use behind the container currently in use.

This container option is applied only to suppliers who are located more than two days from the plant. This kanban container option eliminates the wait time for the empty container to reach the supplier before the replenishment can be filled and shipped back to the manufacturer. This is a good overall container option, especially where perpetuating accurate inventory is an issue. When the container is emptied, it is simply triggered and does not rely on frequent observation, accurate inventory, or accurate on-order conditions.

Kanban Technique 5: Multiple Containers

The multiple container option requires a high degree of maintenance in terms of adjusting the number of kanban cards each time the kanban lot size is recalculated; however, it is second only to the single discrete container option in effectively reducing overall inventory levels.

Environmental Factors for Kanban Technique 5

• Size and volume of part(s) dictates this application.

Application of Kanban Technique 5

This container option is typically employed where the sheer volume and size of the components require many containers. It is used both internally and externally to the plant. The component is assigned a specific physical container size based on the standard quantity (e.g., 100 pieces per container) that each container will carry. The multiple container option does not use a dedicated container because any will do, providing it is the assigned size. When the first piece of material is taken from the container, a trigger occurs, requiring replenishment.

This container option is employed when the sheer volume and size of the component dictates its use. If the kanban lot size was calculated to be 1,050 pieces and there is a standard container quantity per container of 100 pieces (also known as the *multiple*), the 1,050-piece kanban lot size would be increased to 1,100 and the number of containers employed would be (1,100 ÷ 100)11. The next time the kanban lot size calculation takes place, you may have to increase or decrease the number of containers through the number of kanban cards allowed in process. If you were dealing with hundreds or thousands of part numbers using this container application, it would be a huge task to adjust the number of cards manually. In this case, consider an automated adjustment to the number of cards in process.

Design Option 5: Multiple Container Card Option

The multiple container kanban cards are used to signal a need for action, communicate specific part number information, and act as an instrument in controlling the lean manufacturing system. The classic kanban approach employs three distinct types of kanban cards that perform different functions for the multiple container option. An alternative technique using two distinct types of kanban cards can also be employed, and it requires fewer calculations and less maintenance from one planning period to the next.

Kanban Technique 1: Classic Three-Card Multiple Container

The classic kanban approach applies three types of kanban cards for the multiple container application. These kanban cards are the production-ordering card, withdrawal card, and supplier card. (See Appendix C.) For purchased kanban items, the supplier card is employed. If the kanban item is made in-house, each part number will have two cards: the production-ordering card and the withdrawal card. Essentially, if it is made in-house, one calculation determines the number of withdrawal cards and another determines the number of production-ordering cards.

Environmental Factors for Kanban Technique 1

- Multiple containers are employed.
- Continuous improvement is sought in reducing the number of kanban cards.

Application of Kanban Technique 1

In the classic kanban application for multiple containers, three basic kanban cards initiate action based on consumption. The first kanban card is the withdrawal card, which is attached to the containers located at the point of use. (See Figure 4-4.) This kanban card circulates only between the point of use and the cell responsible for replenishment. When consumption first begins on the multiple container option at the point of use, the withdrawal card is removed and placed at a kanban post. From there, the withdrawal cards are taken to the cell responsible for replenishment, based on a pick-up and delivery schedule.

Each withdrawal card authorizes one kanban container of replenishment to be removed from the production outbound area, where ready-made replenishment is staged near the cell responsible for replenishment. The replenishment is transported to the point of use once:

- The withdrawal card is placed on the replenishment container being taken, authorizing its movement.
- The production-ordering card is removed from the outbound replenishment container being removed and placed at its designated kanban post at the cell responsible for replenishment, which is then placed on the production kanban board.

The production-ordering card circulates only within the cell responsible for replenishment and its outbound area, and authorizes production.

The third and final card is the supplier card, which is attached to the full containers located at a work cell inbound area. Once consumption occurs, the supplier card is removed and placed at its designated kanban post. From there, it goes to the central supplier

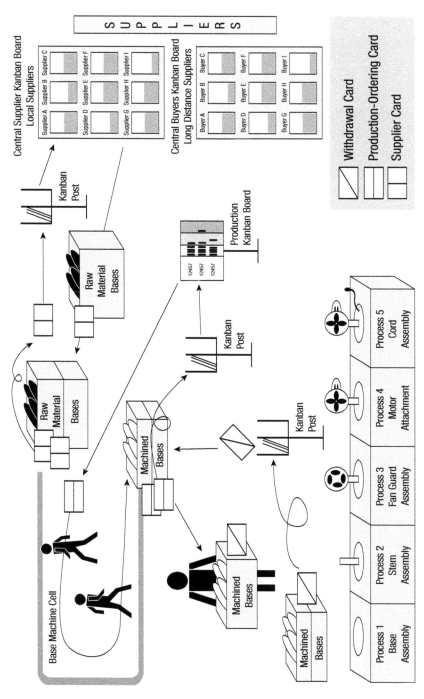

Figure 4-4. Classic three-card multiple container.

kanban board, and then finally to the supplier (local supply base). After the supplier receives the supplier card and fills the standard container with the prescribed replenishment quantity, the supplier places the supplier card in a plastic pouch, attaches it to the replenishment container, and delivers it to the OEM. The card will then be taken to the inbound area.

The key focus of this discussion is the withdrawal card and the production-ordering card. The objective is to remove a small quantity of withdrawal cards or production-ordering cards in circulation (making the number of cards less than the permitted number) to determine root cause issue(s) as to what is preventing the reduction of the number of cards. This way, the specific area targeted for improvement can be studied to lower the number of cards. Segmenting and creating a distinction between the withdrawal card and the production-ordering card highlights root cause issue(s) where improvement is sought (either with production cards or withdrawal cards).

Key Note

Having a distinct card for withdrawal and production creates the need to have two separate kanban lot size calculations for the same part number. There would be one calculation for the withdrawal card and another for the production card.

Kanban Technique 2: Alternative Two-Card Method

An alternative multiple bin card methodology employs a total of two cards, which minimizes the number of kanban lot size calculations and maintenance that need to take place. These two cards are a production-ordering card and a supplier card. The production-ordering card still performs the same function of initiating production but is also used to perform the function of the withdrawal card.

Environmental Factors for Kanban Technique 2

- Numerous part numbers require recalculation; there is a need to minimize maintenance of cards (adding and subtracting) and calculation time.

- Other methods of identifying areas of improvements are employed, including value stream mapping, overall equipment effectiveness calculations, transportation schedule reviews, and Pareto charts.

Application of Kanban Technique 2

The production-ordering card for the multiple bin container option will circulate between the point of use and the cell responsible for replenishment. The work cell outbound area is typically eliminated. When consumption first occurs on the multiple container at the point of use, the production-ordering card is removed and placed on its designated kanban post. From there, the production-ordering card is taken to the cell responsible for replenishment and placed on the kanban post (later placed on the production kanban board). When replenishment is made, the production card is placed back on the container, which is returned to the point of use.

If there is a high degree of commonality of components used in a multitude of different departments, the production card can be bar code scanned, sending the signal to the cell responsible for replenishment. A manufacturing traveler will be produced at the replenishment cell, and it will reflect where the replenishment is to be sent. (See Figure 4-5.) This kanban technique works well with

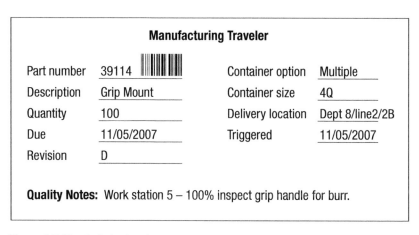

Figure 4-5. Manufacturing traveler.

the multiple container option, because the number of kanban cards in play can be automatically adjusted once the triggered demand is in the computer.

Key Note

The lead time and safety stock associated with the withdrawal card will now be added to the calculation of production-ordering cards.

Design Option 6: Triggering

There is much more involved in triggering than just alerting and communicating the specifics of a need for replenishment. The manner in which triggers occur determines the following:

- Speed in which communicating the need occurs
- Reliability of that communication not having lost kanban cards
- Additional capabilities that can be gained

Kanban Technique 1: Manual Triggering

Manual methodology is employed.

Environmental Factors for Kanban Technique 1

- There is a limited quantity of part numbers.
- The manufacturing plant is relatively small in size and the work is not labor intensive.
- The majority of suppliers are local.
- All items are kanban items (there are no MRP items to blend in).

Application of Kanban Technique 1

- **Supplier card (local suppliers):** The supplier card is removed from the container at the point of use and is placed at the designated kanban post. Collection of these cards is made from various kanban posts located within the plant and placed at the central supplier kanban board that is segmented by suppliers. Local suppliers pick up their respective supplier cards and the empty containers and deliver their current load of replenishment. The supplier, when delivering the replenishment, places the supplier cards in plastic pouches and attaches them to the containers. The containers are then delivered to the point of use.

- **Supplier card (long-distance suppliers):** The long-distance suppliers' kanban cards are distinguished from the local suppliers' kanban cards by color or other attribute. The long-distance supplier card is removed from the container at the point of use and is placed at the designated kanban post. Collection of these cards is made from various kanban posts located within the plant and placed at the central buyer kanban board, segmented by buyer. Buyers collect their respective kanban cards, and phone, fax, or e-mail the supplier for a release while the empty containers are shipped to the respective suppliers. The long-distance supplier card is then taken to receiving and placed in a supplier receipt box segmented by the supplier. The supplier does not receive these cards. The supplier places the part number for each container in the container, and when received, the long-distance supplier kanban cards are removed from the supplier receipt box, placed in plastic pouches, and attached to the containers by the receiving department. The containers are then delivered to the point of use.
- **Production-ordering card (alternative two-card method):** The card is removed from the plastic pouch at the point of use and placed on the kanban post. It is then delivered to the replenishment work cell's kanban post and then to the production kanban board. When production is completed, the production-ordering card is placed back in the plastic pouch, and the containers are taken to the point of use.

This kanban technique is excellent for smaller workshops that are not labor intensive and do not have many part numbers in their system.

Key Notes

1. Lost kanban cards can be an issue.
2. Maintaining a kanban log of the number of kanban cards in play for a multiple-container option and manually adjusting the number of kanban cards in play is typically doable when dealing with less than 100 part numbers.
3. It is difficult to determine the number of hours of work required at each work cell by looking at the production kanban board. It is important to know the hours of work currently triggered at each cell so that they can be staffed appropriately.
4. Single discrete container and single full container options are not typically employed in a manual-triggering environment, because it would be too involved to physically determine the quantity in the container and the quantity on order, and then compare that total to the kanban lot size. This would have to be performed daily, which in most cases is unrealistic.
5. Dual and triple containers for purchased items can be used in a manual-triggering environment. The containers are permanently assigned and have labels affixed to them identifying the part number, point-of-use location, and supplier. The supplier card is placed on or in the container. When the container is empty, the supplier card is removed and follows the same route as discussed above for local and long distance suppliers.
6. The dual container for internally produced items can be used in a manual-triggering environment. The triggered production card and empty container are taken to the cell responsible for replenishment. The production card is placed in the cell's kanban post, which is then placed on the production kanban board. When produced, the production card is placed on the dual container and returned to the point of use. If a high degree of commonality of parts exists throughout the facility, see Kanban Design Option 19.

Kanban Technique 2: Automated Triggering

The automated triggering methodology is employed. Its focus is not only the elimination of the non-value-added activities of the manual-triggering process but also the additional capabilities required for a complex environment that can be attained after the triggered data is in the computer. By placing the triggered data into the computer your system can

- Reflect current triggered load hours for each cell
- Automatically prioritize each cell's triggered items
- Perform material simulations to ensure all the supporting items are available for production prior to commencing production
- Automatically expedite shortages
- Automatically communicate the trigger anywhere in the world immediately
- Automatically adjust the number of kanban cards in play without user intervention
- Simplify the receiving process
- Lend itself to being blended in with MRP released items

All of these points are discussed in Chapters 5 through 7.

Environmental Factors for Kanban Technique 2

- There are hundreds or thousands of part numbers on kanban.
- Suppliers are located locally, throughout the United States, and throughout the world.
- The manufacturing facility is large.
- A mix of kanban and MRP items are employed.

Application of Kanban Technique 2

This technique employs computer monitors at each work cell. Suppliers obtain or are sent their triggered demand electronically (for example, electronic data interchange (EDI), Extranet, FTP server). This technique also employs bar codes, electronic weight scales, and manufacturing/purchasing traveler cards, deduct points, backflushing, as follows:

- **Single discrete—manufacturing:** When the total of on-hand and on-order quantities fall below the kanban lot size, the difference in quantity is automatically triggered by the computer system and placed in a manufacturing queue file for the cell responsible for replenishment. A due date is calculated by the system and is based on the date triggered and the manufacturing lead time (an element of the manufacturing replenishment lead time; see Appendix C), using a manufacturing calendar. The triggered items that are in the manufacturing queue file will appear on the computer monitor of the work cell or production line that is responsible for producing the replenishment. The computer monitors are positioned at the start of the work cell or production line. The computer monitor will reflect a manufacturing queue screen, which shows the part number; description, quantity triggered, and due date for each item in the manufacturing queue file and then sort the items according to the priority rules. When the cell operator selects the next item at the top of the list to be produced from the manufacturing queue screen, a bar-coded manufacturing traveler is printed for that part number. (See Figure 4-5.) The printed manufacturing traveler contains the part number, description, triggered order quantity, due date, revision number, container option, container size, point-of-use delivery location, date triggered, and quality notes. The part number specific bar code can be used to initiate production equipment (for example, auto masking and wave solder machine setup), deduct points, test equipment, and backflush. When the manufacturing traveler is printed, it removes the triggered item from the manufacturing queue file and places it in the manufacturing initiated file. Once the item is produced, it is backflushed and delivered to the point of use. Backflushing removes the quantity produced from the manufacturing initiated file and increases the on-hand inventory.

- **Single full—manufacturing:** Same as the first bullet, except the order quantity equals the full kanban lot size.
- **Dual container—manufacturing:** Same as the first bullet, except the dual container has a bar-coded label affixed to its dedicated container. When the container is empty, it is

scanned, which generates a replenishment order for the full kanban lot size. A printed label is affixed to the container that reflects part number, description, and cell responsible for replenishment and point-of-use location. The empty containers are taken to the cell responsible for replenishment. The produced items are placed in the container and delivered to the point of use.

- **Multiple container—manufacturing:** Same as the preceding bullet, except when a container is first accessed, it is triggered for the standard container quantity. The bar-coded manufacturing traveler residing on the container in a plastic pouch is removed and bar scanned, which generates a replenishment order at the cell responsible for replenishment. Once the item is manufactured, the manufacturing traveler will be placed in a plastic pouch and placed on the container of the just produced item and delivered to the point of use.

- **Single discrete—purchasing:** When the total of on-hand and on-order inventory falls below the kanban lot size, the difference in quantity is automatically triggered and placed in a purchasing hold file. The items in the purchasing hold file at that point in time will reflect the supplier responsible for replenishment, part number, and triggered kanban order quantity. The supplier due date is automatically calculated and provided to the supplier based upon the agreed-on supplier lead time (see Appendix C) at the time the electronic signal is transmitted to the supplier, along with an automatically assigned purchase order number. For example, if today is Wednesday, the scheduled supplier download occurs once a week on Friday, and the agreed-on manufacturing lead time is two manufacturing days, the due date will be calculated to be the following Tuesday, after the download takes place on Friday. Once the supplier begins to perform the scheduled download, a purchase order number will automatically be assigned and the supplier due date determined. The triggered item will then be removed from the purchasing hold file and be placed in the purchasing on-order file. On receipt of the replenishment, a purchasing traveler is generated that reflects whether the part requires inspection, plus any quality notes and the point of use location for delivery. The item received will then automatically be removed from the purchasing on-order file and be reflected as an on-hand quantity.

- **Single full—purchasing:** Same as the preceding bullet, except the order quantity equals the full kanban lot size.
- **Dual container—purchasing:** Same as the preceding bullet, except that the dual container has a bar code label affixed to its part-specific dedicated container. In addition, it has a label affixed to the container reflecting the part number, description, supplier, and point-of-use location. When the container is empty, the container is scanned, which generates the trigger. The empty container is sent to the supplier, who refills the container per the quantity triggered.
- **Triple container—purchasing:** Same as the preceding bullet, except that the supplier already has an empty container and immediately fills and ships it, and the OEM sends the just emptied container to the supplier to use for the next trigger.
- **Multiple container—purchasing:** Same as the preceding bullet, except that when a container is first accessed, the container is triggered for the standard container quantity. The bar-coded purchasing traveler residing on the container in a plastic pouch is removed and bar scanned, which generates a replenishment order. The supplier will use the prescribed container type, place the quantity that was triggered in the container, and ship the container to the OEM. On receipt of the replenishment, a purchasing traveler is generated and placed in a plastic pouch, which is placed on the container.

Fully automating the kanban system for the environment described significantly reduces non-value-added activities, enables immediate reaction to customer needs, significantly reduces operating costs, and enables required capabilities that can be accomplished only through the computer and can, in most cases, be accomplished by using your existing ERP/MRPII package. For more details on fields and files, see my book, *Integrating Kanban with MRPII*, published by Productivity Press. It takes effort and time, but the end result is a powerful system designed to meet the needs of your environment.

Key Notes

1. *Manufacturing kanban items are given due dates based on the date triggered and manufacturing lead time. MRP items that are made in the same cell are also given due dates. In this case, the common denominator of blending MRP items with kanban items is the due date. The due date is what is used to blend MRP and kanban items together when they are made in the same work cell. This is accomplished by having triggered demand in the computer and prioritizing the workload based on the due date. (See Design Option 15 in Chapter 6.)*
2. *Most of the fields are available in most ERP/MRPII systems to accommodate this methodology and can be done in most cases without changing source codes. A few simple routines will need to be written.*

Design Option 7: Alternative Triggering Methods

Kanban comes in many different forms, enabling you to meet the specific needs of your environment. Covered in the following sections are five kanban techniques, each powerful in its own way.

Kanban Technique 1: Broadcast Methodology

The broadcast technique is perhaps the ultimate kanban technique for minimizing inventory.

Environmental Factors for Kanban Technique 1

- Items are too big and or too expensive to keep a predetermined quantity on hand.
- Signal can be sent to a source of supply and stock will be delivered to the point of use before it is needed.

Application of Kanban Technique 1

In the classic methodology, this signal is sent from the start of the production line after production begins on the final product. (See Figure 4-6.) The signal is sent to the work cell or supplier, who is responsible for providing the required item. The item is produced and delivered to the point of use at the assembly line (elapsed time, for example, is 25 minutes) prior to the final assembly reaching that point (accumulated process time, for example, is 30 minutes) in the assembly process.

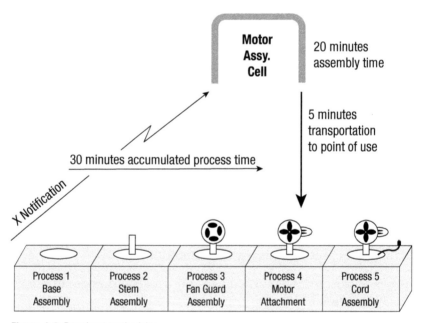

Motor Assembly

Accumulated Process Time = 30 Minutes – Elapsed Time = 25 Minutes

Figure 4-6. Broadcast methodology.

The broadcast methodology is a powerful technique and should be the goal for expensive or extremely large items. A number of adaptations can make this technique more applicable, providing it is within customer delivery expectations. As an example, on the day an item is booked, you can have the signal sent to the cell or supplier. Give the cell or supplier 1 day to complete the item and deliver it to the production line. Initiate the final assembly 2 days after the items are booked. This enables you to significantly reduce inventory on expensive or large items.

Key Notes

All the kanban container options maintain a predetermined quantity of inventory on hand. The broadcast technique, however, maintains no predetermined quantity of inventory on hand and, in most cases, is consumed within a day of the inventory arriving at the point of use.

Kanban Technique 2: Material Card/Signal Card

This technique employs a visual approach to initiating action.

Environmental Factors for Kanban Technique 2

- Excessive setup times are creating a capacity issue.

Application of Kanban Technique 2

In environments that have machines requiring extensive setup time, coupled with capacity issues, apply this technique to minimize the frequency of setup. In these cases, the production quantity has more to do with run frequency than with replenishment lead time. To apply this method, the desired run frequency is greater than the replenishment lead time, and the formula for determining its kanban lot size (used as the order quantity) is:

$$\frac{\text{(average daily demand)} \times \text{(run frequency + safety stock)}}{\text{standard container quantity}}$$

For example, if the average daily demand is 1,000 per day, run frequency is every 30 manufacturing days, zero safety stock, and standard container quantity is 5,000, the kanban lot size would be (1,000) × (30 + 0) ÷ (5,000) = 6 containers. The material card is used to acquire the material that will be used for production, and the signal card is used to authorize the full production of all (i.e.,

6) containers. The signal card and material card are visible on the outside of the totes that house the components, which are stacked on top of each other. The signal card and material card are positioned within the stack of totes, visible to the outside of the container from a timing standpoint. The material card is positioned higher in the stack of totes than the signal card and is therefore initiated first when the tote above it is lifted for consumption. The material card is then taken and placed on a post next to the machine, authorizing the material that is specified on it to be brought to the machine. When the signal card is then freed, it, too, will be taken to the post and hung, authorizing production. (See Figure 4-7.)

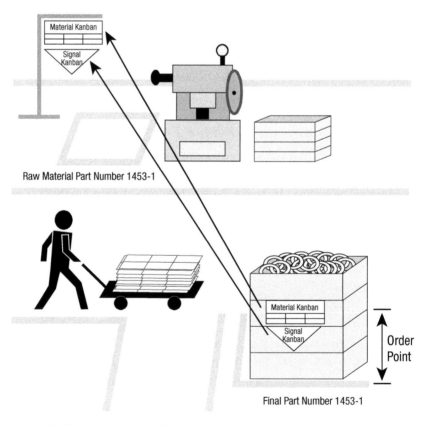

Figure 4-7. Signal card and material card.

The placement of these cards in the stack is based on the following:

- **Signal card:** This card authorizes production. If the replenishment lead time is 10 days, the signal card would be placed on top of the second container from the bottom (1,000 average daily demand) $\times$ (10–days' replenishment lead time + zero days' safety stock) = 10,000 ÷ 5,000 pieces per container = 2 containers. Essentially, this is the order point.
- **Material card:** This card authorizes material to be brought and positioned next to the machine. It is placed above the signal card, based on its lead time to acquire the material and to place it at the point of use. In this example, it takes 5 days, which equals (1,000 average daily demand) $\times$ (5-day lead time) ÷ 5,000 standard container quantity = 1 container. This material card will be placed (2 containers for the signal card + 1 container for the material card) on top of the third container from the bottom.

Kanban Technique 3: Kanban Squares

Kanban squares are used to uniformly pace workers on the assembly line.

Environmental Factors for Kanban Technique 3

- The assembly time for each worker is not exact; that is, it is not balanced. In addition, different work speeds of individual workers create an uneven flow.

Application of Kanban Technique 3

This is a visual technique that is used to uniformly pace operators on the assembly line. A square is placed on the worktable to the left and right of each worker. When the individual worker has finished his or her portion of the assembly, he or she places the item just completed in the square to their right. The individual worker will not begin assembling another unit until the worker on the right removes the unit from that square. When the square to the right of the worker is empty, he or she takes the unit in the square to the left and begins the work, thus authorizing the worker to the left to begin assembling another unit. (See Figure 4-8.)

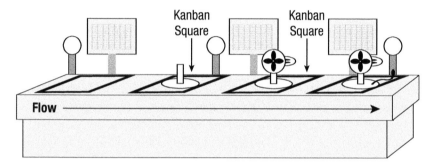

Figure 4-8. Kanban squares.

Kanban Technique 4: Visual Kanban

Visual indicators initiate replenishment. Visual kanban is fairly straightforward in application, but as demand shifts, so must the visual indicators used to initiate action.

Environmental Factors for Kanban Technique 4

- Demand is predicable, rarely fluctuating.
- Visual indicators are next to the point of action.

Application of Kanban Technique 4

This technique can be applied in a variety of ways, such as putting a piece of tape on the wall, and when the stacked containers are below the tape, production is initiated. Another way is that the replenishment cell is connected via conveyor to the final assembly line. A predetermined kanban quantity resides on the conveyor (for example, 3 motors). (See Figure 4-9.) When an item is consumed, this consumption initiates the replenishment cell to replace the 1 item that was consumed. A final example is where a part number is reflected on the floor, and the line behind it is where the replenishment containers reside (within the hash mark of each container). When a container is taken, it is evident that replenishment of 1 container is required.

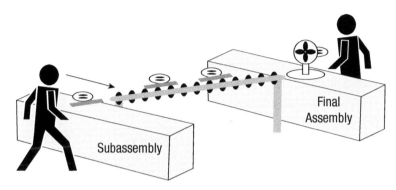

Figure 4-9. Visual kanban.

Kanban Technique 5: Kanban Carts

Kanban carts are an effective means of triggering the need for replenishment and providing the means to transport the replenishment back to the point of use

Environmental Factors for Kanban Technique 5

- Size, volume, or weight of components makes this application desirable. The intent is to simplify the handling and movement.
- This kanban technique is applied only internally to the shop.

Application of Kanban Technique 5

Four-wheeled carts are used in place of the withdrawal card and production-ordering card. The carts are dedicated to a specific part number, which is indicated on the cart. A label on the cart also reflects the standard container quantity, point-of-use location, and cell responsible for replenishment. Once the cart is completely empty at the point of use, it is returned to the cell responsible for replenishment. The empty cart authorizes the replenishment cell to initiate production. After replenishment is made, the cart is delivered back to the point of use with the replenishment. When kanban lot sizes are recalculated, the number of carts are added and subtracted as if they were multiple containers.

Key Notes

Tow motors are frequently used; however, they track dirt throughout the shop, such as from the machine shop to the lacquer department. Instead, utilizing a four-wheel cart with a realistic quantity (and weight) of components contributes to keeping the plant cleaner.

Design Option 8: System Maintenance

The objective of system maintenance is to rapidly and effectively modify the number of kanban cards in process and to reflect the appropriate kanban lot sizes after recalculation takes place. For the single, dual, and triple container options, this means adjusting the kanban lot sizes, and for the multiple container application, the number of cards in process by part number may require adjustment after recalculation. These adjustments, regardless of whether this is a manual or automated system, must be done immediately after recalculation to avert stockouts and inflated inventory levels. There is a manual and automated methodology in performing maintenance, and the appropriate selection is based on the user's specific environmental factors.

Kanban Technique 1: Manual Methodology

A kanban journal or spreadsheet is used to keep track, by part number, of the kanban lot sizes and quantity of kanban containers in play for the multiple container application. This kanban journal or spreadsheet is updated each time kanban lot sizes are recalculated. Physical adjustments to kanban lot sizes and number of containers are then required.

Environmental Factors for Kanban Technique 1

- There is a limited quantity of part numbers on kanban, or numerous part numbers for which the projected demand remains constant.

- Manual kanban lot size calculation method is employed.
- The trigger is performed manually.

Application of Kanban Technique 1

The manual methodology employs a kanban journal or spread-sheet, reflecting the current kanban lot sizes for the dual, triple, and multiple container options. For the multiple container application, the number of cards in process is also reflected. New kanban lot size and changes in the number of containers are put into place in the following manner:

- **Supplier card (local suppliers):** When recalculation of kanban lot sizes takes place, additional cards are placed in the central supplier kanban board if they are to be added for the multiple container application. When cards are to be subtracted for the multiple container application, they are taken from the central supplier kanban board. If cards are not on the central supplier kanban board, they are then looked for at the kanban post, and then finally at the point of use. For dual containers, new kanban cards need to be printed and placed in or on the containers, and the old kanban cards disposed of. If the kanban has been triggered, the search begins on the central supplier kanban board, and then the kanban post. If the kanban item is already in the hands of the supplier, there is no action until receipts are made, at which time the card will be exchanged for one that reflects the new kanban lot size.
- **Supplier card (long-distance suppliers):** When recalculation of kanban lot sizes takes place, additional kanban cards are placed in the central buyer kanban board if they are to be added for the multiple container application. When cards are to be subtracted, they are taken *from* the central buyer kanban board. If cards are not on the central buyer kanban board, they are then looked for at the kanban post, and then finally at the point of use. For triple containers, new kanban cards need to be printed and placed in or on the

containers, and the old kanban cards disposed of. If the kanban has been triggered, the search begins on the central buyer kanban board, and then the kanban post. If the kanban item is already in the hands of the supplier, there is no action until receipts are made, at which time the card will be exchanged for one that reflects the new kanban lot size.

- **Production-ordering card (classic three-card system):** When recalculation of kanban lot sizes takes place, additional cards are placed on the kanban post at the cell responsible for replenishment for the multiple container option. When cards are to be subtracted, they are taken from the production kanban board. If cards are not on the production kanban board, they are then looked for at the kanban post at the cell responsible for replenishment, and then at the outbound area. For dual containers, new kanban cards need to be printed and placed in or on the containers, and the old kanban cards disposed of. If the kanban has been triggered, the search begins on the production kanban board, then at the replenishment cell's kanban post, and then at the point of use kanban post.

- **Withdrawal cards:** When recalculation of kanban lot sizes takes place, additional cards are placed on the kanban post at the point of use for the multiple container option. When cards are to be subtracted, they are taken from the kanban post at the point of use and, if not available, are removed from the containers that have not been triggered at the point of use.

Key Notes

1. *It should be obvious that the manual methodology is a slow and cumbersome process and should not be employed when there are hundreds or thousands of part numbers.*
2. *Typically, when a triggered order has been called in to the supply base, it remains in effect unless a stockout is projected to occur.*
3. *Single container options are not typically employed in this environment.*

Kanban Technique 2: Automated Maintenance

Automate the kanban maintenance process.

Environmental Factors for Kanban Technique 2

- There are hundreds or thousands of part numbers on kanban.
- Kanban lot sizes are automatically calculated.
- The trigger is automatically performed.

Application of Kanban Technique 2

Once the kanban lot sizes and number of containers are automatically calculated, the kanban calculation routine created by the user will automatically update the ERP/MRPII database with the new kanban lot sizes and automatically adjust the number of multiple bin cards that are in process, as follows:

- **Kanban lot size adjustment:** A field in the computer reflects the kanban lot size. It is updated each time recalculation of kanban lot sizes takes place. The single container discrete, single container full, dual and triple container options will automatically have their kanban lot sizes adjusted in the field by the system. For the single container option, the change in kanban lot sizes can immediately trigger new requirements, which is exactly what is needed. For the dual and triple container options, the kanban items that have been triggered and that remain in the purchasing hold file (that is, have not been downloaded to the supplier) or manufacturing queue file (that is, the manufacturing traveler has not been printed) will have their kanban lot sizes automatically adjusted.
- **Multiple container card increase:** The additional cards will automatically be inserted into the purchasing hold file (purchased items) and manufacturing queue file (manufactured items).
- **Multiple container card decrease:** The number of cards required will first be eliminated from the purchasing hold

file and manufacturing queue file. If additional cards are needed and are not available, the balance still required is placed in what is called an *adjustment field* that is part-number specific. When a trigger occurs, the system will first check the Adjustment Field to see whether there is a quantity of cards that still needs to be subtracted. If there is a quantity in the adjustment field, it will be lowered by any new trigger that occurs and will not permit the trigger to reach the purchasing hold file or manufacturing queue file. If there is no balance in the adjustment field, the trigger will be placed in the appropriate purchasing hold file or manufacturing queue file.

Key Notes

1. *Once the manufacturing traveler is printed, the kanban requirement is removed from the manufacturing queue file and appears in a manufacturing initiated file.*
2. *Once the suppliers have acquired their orders from the purchasing hold file, they are removed from the purchasing hold file and become purchase orders appearing in the purchase order file.*

Conclusion

The kanban techniques that you select to meet the needs of your environment are critical in acquiring and maintaining the capability to rapidly respond to consumption and projected shifts in demand. The application of kanban does not guarantee rapid response and lower inventories. The cross-functional team that understands its environment and selects the appropriate kanban techniques knowingly designs these capabilities into the kanban system. Selecting kanban techniques that do not agree with the environment can easily cause excessive transportation cost, continuous overnight shipments, hot lists, shortages, high operational costs, and late customer shipments. Imagine applying a manual multiple container card maintenance methodology to 5,000 part numbers with over 25,000 containers in process. How many days or weeks would it take to adjust all the cards? What would happen in the meantime?

Also, imagine applying a single container discrete methodology to most of your purchased part numbers. How many trucks would be lined up at the receiving door? Would there be enough time in the day to receive and process? How about all the indirect costs? Finally, imagine having 9,000 part numbers on kanban with the demand projected to change 6 days ago. Recalculation and adjustment needed to take place 6 days ago. Your team is still calculating the kanban lot sizes by hand, another team is trying to find the kanban cards to add and subtract, and customers are on the phone wanting to know why their shipment was not received. Everyone is working a lot of overtime. Are more people required, or does this system need to be made more effective?

With the right effort, knowledge of your environment, and selection of the appropriate kanban techniques, you can have a kanban system that will appear to operate by itself, with a greatly reduced inventory and operating cost. In Chapter 5, we cover the kanban design options that deal with receiving, inspection, shipping and material handling.

RECEIVING, INSPECTION, SHIPPING, AND MATERIAL HANDLING

The objective of the kanban system is to obtain what is needed, when it is needed, at the appropriate quantities, and at the least total cost. The least total costs are an important area of consideration when selecting kanban design options that directly affect the receiving, inspection, shipping, and the material-handling functions. Making the right choices can ensure that the operational costs are controlled while significantly lowering inventory and non-value-added activities.

Design Option 9: ABC Classification Application

If the sole objective of the kanban system were to reduce inventory, it could be done at the expense of the business as a whole. As an example, the kanban system could employ the single container discrete option for all part numbers; however, the consequence (for illustration purposes) may mean that we would have to:

- Add two more manufacturing shifts for setups.
- Add two more shifts to perform receiving and inspection.
- Have another shift for accounts payable.
- Quadruple the transportation costs.
- Hire a cadre of material-handling people.

The preceding example is sufficient to make the point that the least total cost is an important consideration when designing the kanban system. What we care about from a receiving, shipping, inspection, and material-handling standpoint is that we do not create a situation in which we are receiving the same inexpensive item frequently, which will significantly inflate our costs of shipping, receiving, inspection, and material handling, while not making a noticeable difference in lowering inventory.

Kanban Technique 1: ABC Codes Lot Sizing

ABC codes are used to identify inexpensive items to minimize the frequency of triggering, shipping, receiving, and material handling.

Environmental Factors for Kanban Technique 1

- ABC classifications pertain to the business where approximately 15 percent of the part numbers are A items that represent 80 percent of the dollars expended, 35 percent of the part numbers are B items that represent 15 percent of the dollars expended, and 50 percent of the part numbers are C items that represent 5 percent of the dollars expended.
- A large number of inexpensive kanban items are procured from the same source.

Application of Kanban Technique 1

There is a tradeoff between inventory levels and transportation and handling costs. Expensive items should ideally be frequently triggered and received, and inexpensive items should be infrequently triggered and received. This way, the overall dollar inventory levels, transportation costs, and handling costs are kept low.

The technique described applies only to the inexpensive C items. The C items will be triggered every day; however, the signal to the supplier, requesting replenishment, will not be sent to the supplier daily. Rather, as an example, the kanban signal to the supplier on triggered items requesting supply will be delayed, grouped, and made available for supplier downloads on extended specific intervals of time. For example, Supplier A handles 800 different gaskets that are C items for the OEM. It is contracted that the supplier will be sent a signal reflecting all the triggered items every 15 manufacturing days. Every 15 manufacturing days, the supplier obtains its signals (via Extranet, EDI, phone, fax, and so on). According to the supplier contract, the supplier will deliver all items 2 days from the date of receiving the signals.

Once the delivery to the OEM takes place, it will take the OEM 1 day to make the receipt and 1 day to deliver the replenishment to the point of use. The replenishment lead time used in the kanban formula for all gaskets is 19 days (15 days to signal, 2 days supplier lead time, 2 days to receive and put away at the point of use). Numerous part numbers of gaskets will be triggered in-house during the course of the 15 manufacturing days but not downloaded to the supplier for 15 manufacturing days. The supplier will receive all the triggered kanban signals that have gathered for 15 days all at once and make one consolidated shipment, thus reducing transportation costs. The OEM receiving and delivering to the point of use will also be a consolidated event. Cost is reduced due to the infrequency of shipping and handling. The extra inventory is minor in comparison to savings of dollars and time.

Key Notes

1. *Safety stock is applied with this technique. The example used zero safety stock to help demonstrate the point.*
2. *A 2-day receipt and put-away time was used to demonstrate the point. In practice, all items should be received and put away the same day the goods hit the door.*
3. *It could be argued that the supplier should be made aware of what is being triggered daily. This can be accommodated, as an example, through the use of an Extranet, through which the supplier can view all the items that have been triggered and are waiting for the authorized download day.*

Design Option 10: Shipping Container Option

Cardboard boxes are used to ship replenished kanban containers to the OEM, and the OEM uses cardboard boxes to send the empty kanban containers to the suppliers. These boxes are expensive and have a cost associated with disposal. However, reusable shipping containers may be employed, thus eliminating the cost of the cardboard boxes and simplifying the shipping and receiving processes.

Kanban Technique 1: Reusable Shipping Containers

It is common for kanban items to be shipped back and forth to the suppliers in cardboard boxes, which are discarded after use. These boxes are expensive, and the costs can be greatly minimized by using reusable shipping containers.

Environmental Factors for Kanban Technique 1

- A large number of kanban items are procured from the same source.
- Cardboard boxes are used to ship product to the OEM, and the OEM ships empty kanban containers in cardboard boxes to the supplier.

Application of Kanban Technique 1

The reusable shipping container is made out of heavy-duty cardboard, can be used numerous times, and can house numerous plastic kanban containers. This shipping container is used to ship the empty kanban containers to the suppliers and is used by the supplier to ship the filled kanban containers back to the OEM. This method simplifies the receiving process, because it eliminates the waste of having to open numerous cartons and later deal with disposal. The reusable-shipping containers have one simple lid that is lifted off, allowing all the containers to simply be picked up and received. This reusable container can further condense the supplier's shipment, because several of these flat 5′ × 5′ × 10′ shipping containers as an example can be banded together.

Design Option 11: Receiving Options

The receiving process must be made as lean as possible so as to immediately receive the incoming supply the same day it arrives. Several different approaches can be applied depending on the environmental factors of the business.

Kanban Technique 1: Selective Part Count

Perform counts only on specific parts or suppliers.

Environmental Factors for Kanban Technique 1

- There are hundreds or thousands of part numbers on kanban.
- Items are highly inexpensive.

Application of Kanban Technique 1

A number of major distribution suppliers who receive supplies from countless manufacturers do not count every single item received. They sample the counts from their suppliers, and based on the accuracy of the counts from these suppliers, they know which suppliers to 100 percent count until the accuracy is greatly improved. Counting is an extremely lengthy process (unless automated, as reflected in the following technique) and can significantly back up the receiving area, creating shortages that should not occur. This approach may be considered for very inexpensive items.

Key Notes

1. Before even attempting to propose this technique, a study should be made on the accuracy of counts from each of your suppliers. If they are not accurate, this should be corrected immediately. Both companies should not be forced to perform the non-value-added task of counting (or inspection).
2. Prior to applying this technique to your facility, ensure that a study is performed based on a long-term 100 percent counting program and that approval from the controller is obtained before proceeding.
3. If this technique is employed, there should always be spot checks to ensure that the counts coming in from the suppliers are still accurate.

Kanban Technique 2: Automated Count and Receipt

The non-value-added activities of the receiving process can be vastly streamlined for kanban items.

Environmental Factors for Kanban Technique 2

- There are hundreds or thousands of part numbers on kanban.
- The size of components is relatively small.

• A dual and or triple kanban container application is employed.

Application of Kanban Technique 2

An electronic scale is hooked up to the MRPII/ERP system, and the weight of the component and the weight of the container is in the system. The dual and triple container has a bar-coded label affixed to it, which contains the part number. The kanban container that is being received is placed on the electronic scale and is scanned, which brings up the purchase order on the computer monitor. The scale automatically receives the weight of the component and the weight of the container from the system and determines the quantity in the container. If the count is within the tolerance of the purchase order quantity, the system will automatically perform the receipt and print out a purchasing traveler that reflects where the container should be taken (either inspection or point of use). If the quantity in the container is short, the system will receive the quantity determined and close out the purchase order.

Design Option 12: Inspection Options

Funneling everything received into inspection creates a bottleneck and a potential for shortages, although the required material is in-house. There are several different techniques that should be considered and selected based on the environmental factors of the business.

Kanban Technique 1: Shopfloor Inspection

The floor personnel visually inspect electronic components.

Environmental Factors for Kanban Technique 1
• The components are electronic.
• Material is stored at the point of use.
• Permanent containers are employed with enlarged picture of components.

Application of Kanban Technique 1

Permanent kanban containers (dual or triple containers) will have an enlarged picture of the component attached. Electronic components are rich with numbers and colors; upon receipt, a purchasing traveler is generated, reflecting where the container will be routed. Once the container is delivered to the appropriate department, the floor personnel will compare the contents to the picture prior to placing the container at the point of use.

Kanban Technique 2: Certified Suppliers

Suppliers are certified on specific items, averting the need for the OEM to perform inspection.

Environmental Factors for Kanban Technique 2

- A purchasing traveler is generated upon receipt.
- Quality performance for each supplier and component is maintained.

Application of Kanban Technique 2

Supplier's components by part number are certified inspection waived. A certification process is put into place that evaluates the:

- Supplier's production process to ensure quality is being produced at the source
- Quality program
- Historical quality performance by part number

Based on this program, certain noncritical items can have their inspection waived when received at the OEM. The MRPII/ERP system is made aware of each component that must be routed to inspection. On receipt, the purchasing traveler will provide the routing, reflecting which parts must go to inspection. The quality department has complete control of the purchasing traveler routing file and can code any item it wishes for inspection, remove any item from inspection, and place quality notes on what to look for (in a section of the purchasing traveler).

Conclusion

The shipping, receiving, inspection, and transportation functions must be examined from a least-total-cost perspective when selecting the specific kanban techniques. Yes, it would be wonderful to bring in only the quantities that are needed, as they are needed. However, the reality is that doing so is often cost prohibitive. Even if cost were not the issue, timing would be a concern—getting all the receipts and multiple inspections of the same item, processed immediately day after day. Typically, the best choice is to bring in what is needed, when needed, in the appropriate quantities.

We also covered various techniques used to streamline receiving and inspection, which is vital to processing everything by the end of each day. A standing rule is to have nothing left in receiving or inspection at the end of each day. This, of course, is easier said than done, unless you minimize the workload in these areas, and the work that remains is automated as much as possible. In Chapter 6, we cover operating kanban in manufacturing.

CHAPTER **6**

OPERATING KANBAN IN A
MANUFACTURING ENVIRONMENT

Typically, literature reflecting the simplicity of kanban indicates that the manufacturing floor receives the triggered kanban card, which is placed visually on the production kanban board, and then the part is produced. Unfortunately, this leaves much to the imagination, such as the following:

- How do you determine and plan for future capacity requirements?
- How do you know, by hours, what the current triggered load is at each cell so as to enable the rapid deployment of cross-functional workers to the appropriate work cells, especially in large plants?
- How do you blend the kanban and material requirement planning (MRP) items (not all part numbers can or should be placed on kanban) at the production line or work cells?
- Should you check all the supporting material to ensure supporting material availability prior to initiating the build for final product or assemblies?
- How do you expedite the shortages in the most effective manner for your environment?
- Will all the supporting material fit at the point of use, or will you retain the stockroom or warehouse? If retained, how does the kanban system function?
- Where do you store the components that are common to the plant as a whole and how do you trigger those requirements?

These are all important questions that must be asked and answered during a complete kanban design process. This chapter contains ten design options that answer the preceding questions.

Design Option 13: Manufacturing Capacity Planning

In order for a kanban system to function as designed, the internally triggered replenishment order must be made within replenishment lead time. The replenishment lead time is what is used to determine the kanban lot size. If there is not enough capacity to meet the projected needs of the environment, shortages will occur, and with too much capacity, excessive costs will be incurred. Although kanban is an exceptionally powerful execution tool, it is totally void of planning tools. Nonetheless, the correct levels of capacity must be planned for in advance. The length in time planned must be equal to the time to acquire the necessary resources, be it labor, machines, or buildings. There are several techniques that can be used to plan in the long range, medium range, and short range. A given environment may employ some or all of these techniques, depending on its individual needs.

Kanban Technique 1: Rough-Cut Capacity Planning

Rough-cut capacity planning typically focuses on critical resources to determine whether additional capability is required. Critical resources may include highly utilized specialized machinery or work centers that require special skills.

Environmental Factors for Kanban Technique 1

- Product offerings are limited in scope, and service parts are not a major factor in the business, permitting a nonautomated approach.
- There are only a handful of critical resource areas.
- A rough-cut capacity bill of material and master production schedule can be constructed.

Application of Kanban Technique 1

Rough-cut capacity planning is typically applied manually or employs a simple spreadsheet program. It can be used to determine long- and medium-range capacity requirements. A master production schedule is made, encompassing current sales orders and forecasted demand of end products by month, going out far enough in time to acquire the necessary resources. A rough-cut capacity bill of material is constructed, which reflects, by work center, the amount of direct-labor hours or machine hours required to produce one item. The quantities in the master production schedule, by time period, are then multiplied by the capacity bill of material direct-labor hours or machine hours to determine projected required hours. The projected required hours are then compared to current capacity levels. The difference in the hours represents the action that must be taken. The current capacity hours must reflect the actual amount of time the resource is employed making the product (breaks and planned downtime are factored out). See Figure 6-1 for an example that reflects cross-functional workers and a plant view of projected required hours versus current capacity. The same approach is applied to critical machines.

Key Notes

1. This analysis is normally performed on the production lines, work centers, or specific machines that are considered critical.
2. Bear in mind that this is a rough cut which does not take into consideration service parts, time phasing, lot sizing, or the amount of inventory that may already be on hand.

Kanban Technique 2: Capacity Requirements Planning Module

The capacity requirements planning module is a key component of most MRPII/ERP packages. It is fairly detailed in its determination of required capacity by time period as compared to present capacity.

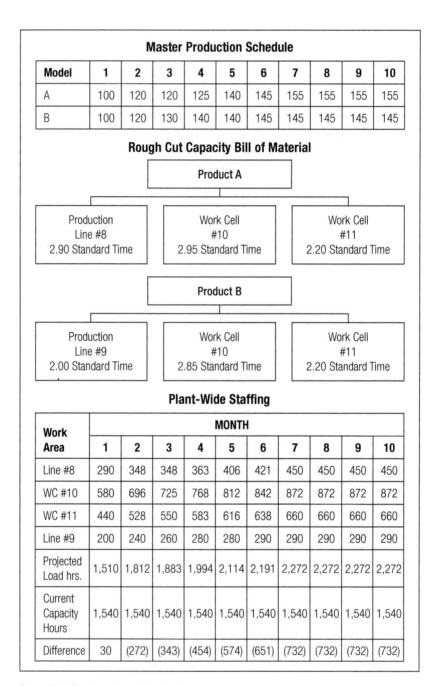

Master Production Schedule

Model	1	2	3	4	5	6	7	8	9	10
A	100	120	120	125	140	145	155	155	155	155
B	100	120	130	140	140	145	145	145	145	145

Rough Cut Capacity Bill of Material

Product A

Production Line #8 2.90 Standard Time	Work Cell #10 2.95 Standard Time	Work Cell #11 2.20 Standard Time

Product B

Production Line #9 2.00 Standard Time	Work Cell #10 2.85 Standard Time	Work Cell #11 2.20 Standard Time

Plant-Wide Staffing

Work Area	MONTH									
	1	2	3	4	5	6	7	8	9	10
Line #8	290	348	348	363	406	421	450	450	450	450
WC #10	580	696	725	768	812	842	872	872	872	872
WC #11	440	528	550	583	616	638	660	660	660	660
Line #9	200	240	260	280	280	290	290	290	290	290
Projected Load hrs.	1,510	1,812	1,883	1,994	2,114	2,191	2,272	2,272	2,272	2,272
Current Capacity Hours	1,540	1,540	1,540	1,540	1,540	1,540	1,540	1,540	1,540	1,540
Difference	30	(272)	(343)	(454)	(574)	(651)	(732)	(732)	(732)	(732)

Figure 6-1. Rough-cut capacity planning.

Environmental Factors for Kanban Technique 2

- There are numerous product offerings; service parts may or may not be a major factor in the business.
- A MRP module, plus bills of material, routings, standard hours, and shop scheduling module are available; a master production schedule can be constructed.

Application of Kanban Technique 2

This technique is performed automatically by the system after the master production schedule is made, exploded through MRP, back scheduled through the shop scheduling module, and interfaced with the capacity planning module. It can be used for long-, medium-, and short-range capacity planning. For long-range capacity planning, a master production schedule, with monthly time buckets, is typically constructed that encompasses current sales orders and forecasted demand of end products, going out in time far enough necessary to acquire the required resources (for example, machines, and direct labor). The master production schedule will also include expected service part sales. An MRP module is exploded, using the master production schedule. MRP will go gross to net level by level, utilizing the bill of material, and will perform lot sizing and offsetting. The output of MRP is used by the shop scheduling module to back schedule MRP's output, utilizing the routings and standards to determine both labor and machine capacity requirements. The output from the capacity requirements planning module for long-range planning will be summarized by month and then compared (by work center and the plant as a whole) with the projected load hours to current capacity hours for both labor and machines.

Key Note

The output is used to plan capacity; it is not used to drive the shop.

Kanban Technique 3: Production Line Staffing

This is a straightforward method of determining staffing requirements for the final product production line.

Environmental Factors for Kanban Technique 3

- The master production schedule is load-smooth.
- Product offerings are limited in scope, permitting a nonauto-mated approach.

Application of Kanban Technique 3

This kanban technique can be applied automatically by the system or be manually performed and used for short-range capacity planning. There are three main elements required to determine the planned staffing levels of the final product production line:

- **Takt time:** This sets the pace of production. Takt time is the required production output rate (expressed as an average output time per unit) that must be completed in order to produce the stated daily production quantities. For example, 1 unit must be completed every 14 seconds.
- **Production line effective time:** This is the amount of time each day that the production line is producing product. Subtract lunch, breaks, and other activities such as autonomous maintenance, cleaning, group improvements, and so on.
- **Labor content per unit:** This is the standard time per unit. In other words, this is the labor content required, expressed as the time it takes to make 1 unit: for example, 56 seconds of labor per unit.

To arrive at the final assembly production line staffing levels the takt time must first be computed by determining how many units need to be produced per day and dividing that into the production line effective time per day. Then, the labor content per unit is divided by the takt time. (See Figure 6-2.)

Kanban Technique 4: Flexible Work-Cell Staffing Requirements

This approach is used to determine anticipated staffing levels for flexible work cells. When demand is projected to shift, the staffing levels for flexible work cells are recalculated.

Model	Planned Production for 20 Day Period
B54687	10,100
C47562	12,100
G75786	16,200
	38,400 total final product units to be built in 20 day period = 1,920 final product units required per day. Production line effective time per day = 448 minutes = 26,880 seconds per day. 26,800 seconds per day / 1,920 units required per day = 14 seconds takt time. 56 seconds labor content / 14 second takt time = 4 people required

Figure 6-2. Final product line staffing requirements.

Environmental Factors for Kanban Technique 4

- There is a load-smooth master production schedule.
- Flexible work cells are employed.

Application of Kanban Technique 4

This kanban technique is typically applied to short-range capacity planning. It can either be applied automatically by the system or manually performed. Three main elements are required to determine the planned staffing requirements of work cells:

- **Average daily demand:** This is the projected daily amount that is expected to be required each day. For example, the average daily demand for part number 12323 is 948, part number 34543 is 700, and part number 56546 is 400. (See Figure 6-3.)
- **Labor content per unit:** The labor content per unit encompasses setup time, processing labor time, and move time. For example, the labor content per unit for part number 12323 is 0.75, part number 34543 is 0.60, and part number 56546 is 0.50.

- **Operator effective time per day:** The operator effective time per day is the amount of time the operator is producing product. To determine this, take the total time the operator is onsite (typically 8 hours) and subtract lunch, breaks, and other activities such as autonomous maintenance and clean up. For this example, we use an operator effective time per day of 450 minutes.

Flexible Work Cell Staffing Requirements Work Cell 8 – Coupling Machining				
Part Number	Description	Average Daily Demand	Labor Content Per Unit	Extended Total
12323	Coupling 5″	948	0.75	711 Minutes
34543	Coupling 7″	700	0.60	420 Minutes
56546	Coupling 8″	400	0.50	200 Minutes
				1,331 Minutes per day / 450 operator effective time = 2.95 people. Round up. = 3 people required

Figure 6-3. Flexible work-cell staffing requirements.

The labor content per unit is multiplied by the average daily demand for each item produced in the cell, and then is totaled. This total is then divided by the operator effective time to determine the number of people required for the work cell.

When it comes to planning capacity, it is often best to carry more capacity rather than less. The additional capacity provides manufacturing the flexibility required to respond to unexpected demand.

Design Option 14: Monitoring Current Triggered Load

Planning capacity based on anticipated demand is important in ensuring that the required resources are available. However, in day-to-day operations, you need to know the actual triggered load that is present for each production line and work cell in order to shift the required number of workers to the appropriate flexible work cells and to apply overtime where required. Some manufacturing environments are small in size, and the quantity of part numbers on kanban is limited, while other environments are extremely large in size and have hundreds or thousands of part numbers on kanban. The environmental factors dictate the specific kanban technique that is put into place to monitor and react to the current triggered load.

Kanban Technique 1: Visual Load Monitoring

Kanban cards being triggered would be of little value if they were not visible. The kanban cards that are triggered are made visible to provide some form of priority and general understanding of the workload.

Environmental Factors for Kanban Technique 1

- The plant is small in size.
- The quantity of part numbers on kanban is small.
- The volume of business remains within the boundaries of what was planned.
- Manual triggering is employed.

Application of Kanban Technique 1

A kanban production board is employed where the production ordering cards are placed. (See Figure 6-4.) By looking at the board, a fair assessment of current load can be determined. A simple walk through the facility, looking at the kanban boards, will result in a rough determination of staffing requirements. In addition, the kanban production board can provide manufacturing prioritization information based on the number of kanban cards per part number that have been triggered in relationship to the notations on the board.

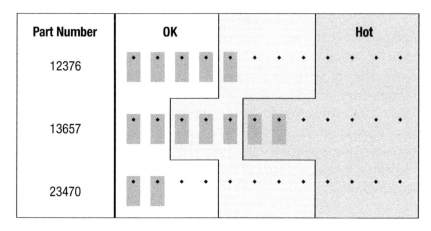

Figure 6-4. Kanban production board.

Key Notes

1. *In environments where the volume shifts, the notations on the board will have to change when the volume changes.*
2. *The more part numbers are handled by the production line or work cell, the less effective this methodology becomes.*
3. *When the final product is able to be built to a load-smooth master production schedule or sequenced schedule, there is less speculation about what the triggered load may look like at each cell each day. The farther away one gets from building to a load-smooth master production schedule or sequenced schedule (such as reacting to customer demand), the greater the need to know the workload in hours at each production line and work cell.*

Kanban Technique 2: Automated Load Hour Monitoring

This method is highly effective in prioritizing the triggered requirements and determining the actual load in hours by work cell. With one summarized report, the workload for all work cells can be displayed, enabling a fast response in shifting cross-functional workers to the appropriate work cells.

Environmental Factors for Kanban Technique 2

- The plant is large.

- The quantity of part numbers on kanban is in the hundreds or thousands.
- The final product build is not load-smooth and frozen; business reacts to unexpected customer demand; and forecasts are not 100 percent accurate.
- Volume changes frequently.
- Automated triggering is employed.

Application of Kanban Technique 2

This environment is complex yet can be handled in an effective manner. Manual methodologies coupled with visual controls are not the answer for this type of environment, because triggered load hours must be known without guesswork. This technique is used in conjunction with automated triggering. When a kanban is triggered, it is automatically placed into the system by scanning the bar code of the triggered container or kanban card, or by the system monitoring the total of on-hand and on-order quantity and comparing it to the kanban lot size. In either case, once triggered, the requirement will appear on the computer monitor at the head of each work cell or production line. (See Figure 6-5.) Each triggered item on the screen reflects the part number, description, quantity triggered, and calculated due date based on manufacturing lead time, plus extended labor hours for each item triggered and total load by day. (See Figure 6-6.) It also reflects a material simulation to determine material availability. This permits the work cell to avoid making items that will encounter a shortage. Some work cells are quite large (for example, as many as 30 workers and 2,000 part numbers staged at the point of use), and this technique is invaluable in preventing partially completed assemblies from sitting and waiting for the balance of material to arrive. A summary report is also made from the available data, reflecting the triggered load for each production line and work cell. (See Figure 6-7.) This enables a quick overview of the triggered load at each flexible work cell so as to reposition the workforce as required. More advanced application involves self-directed work teams that review the reports several times a day and shift themselves to

Figure 6-5. Automated load hour monitoring.

the appropriate areas. When an item is selected to be run, a bar-coded manufacturing traveler is printed, authorizing the specific item and quantity to be produced. Once the manufacturing traveler is printed, the triggered item is automatically removed from the manufacturing queue file and placed in the manufacturing initiated file. Once the item is completed, the triggered item is removed from the manufacturing initiated file and becomes on-hand inventory.

Plant Triggered Load Report					11/07/2007		
Cell Number	11/7/2007	Required Staffing	Maximum Staffing	Issue	11/08/ 2007	11/09/ 2007	Total
5A	35 Hours	4.7	5		15 Hours	3 Hours	53 Hours
5B	42 Hours	5.6	7		16 Hours	7 Hours	65 Hours
5C	61 Hours	8.1	6	*	39 Hours	18 Hours	118 Hours
5D	15 Hours	2.0	4		4 Hours	2 Hours	21 Hours
5E	39 Hours	5.2	6		12 Hours	5 Hours	56 Hours
TOTAL	192 Hours	25.6			86 Hours	35 Hours	313 Hours

Figure 6-7. Plant triggered load report.

Manufacturing Queue Screen

Department 10

11/05/2007

Part Number	Description	Qty Due	Flag	Trigger Date	Due Date	Time Due	Part Status	Hours Loaded
5725649	Bevel Assembly	80	*	11/01/07	11/05/07	0800	OK	17.0 Hours
4275349	Anvil Assembly	50		11/01/07	11/05/07	0826	OK	12.0 Hours
3473274	Jack Assembly	35		11/02/07	11/05/07	0900	Short 100%	4.0 Hours
7325643	Spindle Assembly	100		11/02/07	11/05/07	1800	Short CM 56	18.0 Hours
								51.0 Hours Total

Department 10

11/06/2007

Part Number	Trigger Description	Due Qty Due	Time Flag	Part Date	Hours Date	Due	Status	Loaded
5268732	Lever Assembly	80		11/02/07	11/06/07	0800	OK	22.0 Hours
6758456	Shim Assembly	50		11/02/07	11/06/07	0826	OK	10.0 Hours
1896545	Bracket Assembly	35		11/01/07	11/06/07	0900	OK	4.0 Hours
3276908	Grip Assembly	100		11/02/07	11/06/07	1800	OK	16.0 Hours
								52.0 Hours Total

*Any item simulated to be short will have an asterisk and be moved to the top automatically

Figure 6-6. Manufacturing queue screen.

Design Option 15: Manufacturing Prioritization

When a production line or work cell is responsible for more than one part number, the need will arise to determine the sequence in which to build. The method employed is dependent on the environmental factors as demonstrated in this section.

Kanban Technique 1: First In–First Out

The first item triggered is the first item produced.

Environmental Factors for Kanban Technique 1

- The production line is load-smooth and sequenced.
- The work cell is physically located next to the final production line, where there is no delay in receiving the replenishment signal.
- The work cell is not serving two or more production lines.
- The work cell predominately produces kanban items (with a low number of MRP items).
- The work cell setup time and cycle time through the cell is short and able to respond to the consumption rate of the production line.

Application of Kanban Technique 1

The triggered requirements at the replenishment work cell immediately reflect the sequence and quantities consumed by the final production line. The replenishment work cell is able to match replenishment rate with consumption rate. The supporting cell will build to a first in, first out method. In other words, the sequence in which the cards arrive is the sequence in which they will be built.

Kanban Technique 2: Sequence Chart

The work cell will build in the order of the final assembly-sequence chart.

Environmental Factors for Kanban Technique 2

- The final assembly production line is load-smooth and sequenced.
- The work cell is not serving two or more production lines.
- The work cell is located at a distance to the final assembly line where there is a delay in receiving the replenishment signal.
- The work cell produces predominately kanban items (a low number of MRP items).
- The work cell setup time and cycle time through the cell is short and able to respond to the consumption rate of the production line.

Application of Kanban Technique 2

The timing in which the triggered requirements are received at the replenishment work cell is delayed. The production ordering cards received by the replenishment work cell are placed in order by the final assembly-sequence chart (which reflects the order of the final assembly build; for example, ABACA).

Kanban Technique 3: Automated Availability Ratio

In a number of environments, what dictates the sequence of which item is built is based upon which item is most likely to stockout.

Environmental Factors for Kanban Technique 3

- The master production schedule is not frozen (responds to customer demand).
- The work cell supports more than one production line.
- The work cell is responsible for hundreds of different items.
- The work cell produces predominately kanban items (a low number of MRP items).
- The manufacturing lead time through the cell for most items is approximately the same.
- Automated triggering is applied.
- Automated load-hour monitoring is applied.

Application of Kanban Technique 3

This environment may apply an availability ratio. The *availability ratio* is the ratio between the kanban lot size and the quantity that is on hand. For example, if we had three items on kanban (part number Q, R, and S) and the kanban lot size for Q was 100 with 80 units/pieces on hand, R kanban lot size was 100 with 40 units/pieces on hand, and S kanban lot was also 100 with 10 units/pieces on hand, the availability ratio of Q would be 80 ÷ 100 = 0.80, R = 40 ÷ 100 = 0.40, and S = 10 ÷ 100 = 0.10. The triggered workload is stratified by the lowest availability ratio to the highest. In other words, the work cell would run the lowest availability ratio first, which would be S, and then R, and then Q. Although Q may have been triggered first, its needs are not the greatest. The rationale is that the greatest exposure to stockout would be S, and then R, and then Q. This technique can also be applied to the production line, where finished goods are being run on kanban.

Kanban Technique 4: Due Date

When kanban is triggered, a due date can be determined based on the date triggered and manufacturing lead time. This may be required if MRP items share the same resources as kanban items.

Environmental Factors for Kanban Technique 4

- There is a large mixture of MRP items and kanban items.

Application of Kanban Technique 4

This technique is highly versatile. When a kanban is triggered, its due date is calculated based on the date triggered and the manufacturing lead time. The due date is the common denominator when working in an environment that has both MRP items and kanban items being produced in the same production line or work cell, because MRP items are driven by due date. The workload is therefore stratified by due date.

Design Option 16: Material Availability

Unfortunately, shortages do occur, but this situation should never be viewed as acceptable or normal—the root cause issue(s) need to be identified and rectified. The degree to which they occur is predicated on the:

- Soundness of the kanban design and implementation
- Level to which lean manufacturing has been implemented
- Strength of the supply chain and degree of elimination of non-value-added activities providing reaction capability
- Predictability of final product offerings from a forecasting standpoint
- Degree of linearity
- Methodology in place to identify and to eliminate potential shortages prior to their occurrence

There are two lines of defense against shortages:

- The first is during the automated kanban lot calculation process, where a simulation routine may determine whether the calculated kanban lot size will stockout. If the stock out is projected to occur beyond lead time, the kanban lot size will automatically be adjusted to compensate. If it is projected to occur within lead time, a flag will be raised for user intervention.
- The second is knowing the availability of supporting materials prior to releasing triggered items to be built. If a pending shortage of a supporting item can be identified when its parent is triggered, reaction time is available to attempt to avert the potential shortage before it occurs.

Shortages create numerous problems, especially when they occur in a production line, subassembly, or assembly work cell. Shortages generate additional non-value-added activities and disorganization, because the partially assembled items must be set off to the side and monitored for the shortage to be received. The availability of supporting components and materials should be known prior to initiating production on a triggered demand item. Two kanban techniques are used to accomplish this. One is visual; the other is automated and is covered in the following section.

Kanban Technique 1: Visual

Prior to building a triggered item, the supporting items can be viewed quickly to determine whether all the material is available.

Environmental Factors for Kanban Technique 1

- Each work cell or production line makes only a few items.

Application of Kanban Technique 1

The containers of the supporting materials for a specific model or assembly are given a unique color. Common part numbers are also given their own unique color. A quick visual scan can detect shortage issues and avert the start of the particular triggered item.

Kanban Technique 2: Automated Material Availability Simulation

In environments that have hundreds or thousands of supporting items, an automated approach may be necessary to ensure that all supporting items are available for the parent that is triggered.

Environmental Factors for Kanban Technique 2

- Hundreds or thousands of supporting components are involved.
- On-hand inventory is accurate.
- Bills of material are available and accurate.
- Automated triggering is applied.
- Automated load-hour monitoring is applied.
- Automated prioritization is applied.
- Deduct points and backflushing are applied.

Application of Kanban Technique 2

This kanban technique is normally applied to production lines or work cells that are responsible for producing a wide assortment of items and require hundreds or thousands of supporting materials. In this environment, it is difficult to look at supporting materials bins and ascertain whether there is enough inventory available. In these cells, a number of triggered items are in process ahead of the one you are considering producing, and they may require the same supporting items. Also bear in mind that these cells are typically large due to the quantity of point-of-use materials. Visually determining the availability of supporting materials prior to the initiation of each triggered item to be produced creates an enormous degree of non-value-added activities. The automated material availability simulation uses the computer, especially because the system knows what has been triggered, the priority in which triggered items will be built, what items are in process and their current location, the bills of material for each item triggered, and the on-hand inventory available. The computer can communicate to the user its findings of the supporting material availability via the manufacturing queue screen displayed on the computer monitor at the head of the production line or work cell. (See Figures 6-5 and 6-6.) The computer will display next to each item triggered, under the heading Part Status, whether the material is available to support production. There are three possible levels of status under that heading that can be displayed next to the part number that needs to be produced.

- **OK,** which means all the supporting material should be available
- **Short 100%,** which means nothing can be made
- **Short CM,** which means that there will be a shortage, but a partial quantity can be made. The partial quantity will be specified after the CM (CM = Can Make).

If all the material is available, the cell operator will select it and a bar-coded manufacturing traveler will be generated, authorizing its build. If it says "Short" the bar-coded label cannot be generated unless overridden by the production line or cell lead. This methodology also employs deduct points and backflushing, which provides accurate on-hand inventory information to the material availability routine and provides the location of in-process assemblies that will require additional materials.

The automated material simulation is a routine that will do the following:

- Take the current on-hand inventory balance that is in the containers (deduct points have already been subtracted from the on-hand quantity; the amount has been consumed but is still being produced).
- Acquire the manufacturing initiated file for those items being built and subtract the components still required to complete the build.
- Acquire the manufacturing queue file of the triggered items for what is to be released for build by the priority sequence presented. It will then explode through the bill of material one item at a time from top to bottom using the priority sequence for each triggered item, subtracting what is required from the remaining on-hand inventory. If all the material is available, the system will note "OK" next to the triggered item in the computer. If any material is short, the system will note "Short CM" next to the triggered item and will specify the partial quantity that can be built. It will continue subtracting the inventory as it goes through each triggered item that is to be built, until it reaches the distance in time set by the user. This can tie into an automated expedite routine.

Key Notes

1. *The length of time for which the simulation should look ahead should not be greater than a day; the time is often set to look ahead only a few hours.*
2. *The capabilities listed in the preceding sections typically do not require changing the source code for most systems. These capabilities are routines that are added on to the current system, which simply extracts information that is currently available (for example, on-hand quantity) and applies it to perform the required functions.*

3. *True, creating such a system is a lot of work. But consider the alternative: line shortages, partially made assemblies lying around with notes of what is short attached; clutter; hired expediters to run around and create a shortage list of required materials. With the system in place, you'll be in a position to avert the shortage. Moreover, it will take less time to put this routine in place than to deal with all the mayhem described above.*

Design Option 17: Expediting Supporting Material

Once it is determined that the triggered demand will encounter a shortage, the objective is to acquire the material prior to initiating production of the triggered item. Two kanban techniques can be employed to perform the expedite function; the selection is predicated on the environmental factors.

Kanban Technique 1: Manual Expedite

When shortages are expected or occur, a list is made and expedited by the expediters.

Environmental Factors for Kanban Technique 1

- This environment handles few supporting part numbers.
- This is a manual kanban system.

Application of Kanban Technique 1

When dealing with only a handful of part numbers, a manual method of creating a shortage list and expediting is doable. Automating this process in this environment would have little to no payback.

Kanban Technique 2: Automated Expedite Routine

The automated expedite routine uses the material availability simulation to develop a buyer pending shortage list for purchased items and notifies the manufacturing cell responsible for replenishment of the pending shortage. This information is sent to the responsible parties via the computer system. The responsible parties then key into the system the commitment date and time when the pending shortage items will become available. The commitment date and time can appear on the manufacturing queue screen of the production line or work cell requiring the item.

Environmental Factors for Kanban Technique 2

- You are dealing with hundreds or thousands of part numbers.
- Automated triggering is applied.
- Automated load monitoring is applied.
- Automated prioritization is applied.
- Automated material availability simulation is applied.

Application of Kanban Technique 2

- **Manufactured-supplied material:** The anticipated shortage data from the automated material availability simulation is used in the automated expedite activity. The required replenishment already triggered at the respective work cells will automatically have an asterisk placed next to the triggered items part number that is simulated to be short. Regardless of the specific prioritization method that is in place for supporting manufactured items, the asterisk automatically moves the required item to the top of the prioritization list. The cell responsible for replenishment will then input into the system an expected delivery date and time. This expedited information can appear on the manufacturing queue screen of the production line or work cell requiring the item, next to the part number that is projected to be short.
- **Supplier-supplied material:** The anticipated shortage data from the automated material availability simulation is used in the automated expedite activity. All supplier-related items that are projected to be short will be sorted by responsible buyer and then by supplier, and an expedited list will be generated for the buyer. Each buyer will expedite his or her

respective items and input into the system the date and time of expected arrival. This expedited information will appear on the manufacturing queue screen of the production line or work cell requiring the item, next to the part number projected to be short.

Key Notes

1. *The objective of an effective expedite is to obtain the required items prior to the shortage occurring and to perform this function with minimal non-value-added activities.*
2. *Consideration for automation must have a payback. Typically, this is easily achieved if you are dealing with hundreds or thousands of part numbers.*

Design Option 18: Positioning Material

The most effective storage point of kanban items is the point of use. Storing the same material in a multitude of areas, such as production outbound area, stockroom or warehouse, or overflow racks, creates a number of difficulties and non-value-added activities. The main issues are lack of control in maintaining accurate inventory counts and the non-value-added activities of performing multiple trips to acquire replenishment. Ideally, all the material of a given item will be housed at the point of use, but this may not be possible due to the size and volume of the components. Plus, there is a tradeoff, because the more material that is stored at the point of use, the longer the production line or work cell must be to accommodate this material, which can generate production inefficiencies. This is especially true in work cells where the item being built is physically walked through the cell versus a conveyor-belt-driven production line. This kanban design option is explored in this section to determine the best technique for the specific environment.

Kanban Technique 1: Point of Use

All of the supporting material is positioned at the point of use.

Environmental Factors for Kanban Technique 1

- The volume and size of components equaling the kanban lot size can be accommodated at the point of use.
- There is a low degree of commonality of component to other departments.

Application of Kanban Technique 1

Floor and line space is not an issue. When an item is triggered for replenishment, manufacturing produces it and delivers the replenishment directly to the point of use. When supplier material is received, it, too, is delivered directly to the point of use.

Kanban Technique 2: Overflow Racks

The production lines and work cells that cannot accommodate all of the material at the point of use employ a rack where the excess material is placed.

Environmental Factors for Kanban Technique 2

- Not all the supporting material equaling the kanban lot size can be accommodated at the point of use.
- There is a low degree of commonality of component to other departments.

Application of Kanban Technique 2

This is the next best choice due to the short distance to acquire replenishment, and this technique keeps the responsibility of accurate inventory to one location. Each work cell or production line has its own overflow rack. The overflow rack is positioned as close as possible to the manufacturing cell. When part numbers can have their kanban containers positioned at the point of use, they do; items that cannot should have a smaller subordinate container residing at the point of use with the quantity of material that can be accommodated. The subordinate containers seek their replenishment from the master containers in the overflow rack. The master containers are then triggered for replenishment and delivered to the overflow rack.

Kanban Technique 3: Stockroom/Warehouse

The stockroom or warehouse holds material. The production lines and work cells seek their replenishment from the stockroom or warehouse.

Environmental Factors for Kanban Technique 3

- Manufacturing floor space is highly limited.
- Material consumes too much floor space due to size and or volume.

Application of Kanban Technique 3

There are several approaches to this application, and more than one can be applied to a given facility based on the unique profile of the individual component.

- **Line-side inventory:** This is a calculated predetermined quantity that resides at the point of use, whose replenishment comes from master containers stored in the stockroom or warehouse. The line side is replenished directly from the master containers stored in the stockroom or warehouse. The master containers are triggered based on their consumption supporting line-side replenishment. For this application, the kanban lot size is calculated for both the line-side inventory and the master containers that reside in the stockroom or warehouse.
- **Sequence schedule:** All the material is received and stored in the stockroom or warehouse. The material is sequenced there according to production line requirements and is delivered to the point of use according to the signal.
- **Broadcast:** The *broadcast method* can send a signal to either a work cell or to the stockroom or warehouse for supply. When a final product item begins its assembly process, a signal is sent to the stockroom or warehouse to deliver the signaled items to the point of use. The material is then positioned at the point of use prior to its being required by the final assembly item.

Key Notes

1. The materials on the overflow rack should be able to be acquired without mechanical assistance.
2. Care should be taken as to the weight of any container to ensure that injury does not occur, especially when racking is employed.
3. The material stored on the overflow rack normally has a permanent location assigned, and its location is labeled with the part number.
4. Without question, this approach is the last choice. It contains a great deal of non-value-added activity to calculate and maintain line-side inventory and a master container as well as frequent rehandling of material.

Design Option 19: Common Component Placement

The fewer locations in a facility that a part number has, the easier it is to maintain an accurate inventory count, take corrective action on count discrepancies, perform the kanban lot size calculation, and perform kanban maintenance. The more locations in which a given part number is stored, the more work is involved. Although the objective is to have only one point-of-use location for all materials, it is usually not totally possible, because there is often a high degree of commonality of part numbers between different product lines being manufactured in different locations within the facility. This is especially true for inexpensive items like hardware. In the following sections, we explore the various kanban techniques that can be employed to deal with commonality of part numbers.

Kanban Technique 1: Central Location

Centrally locate common part numbers employing master containers.

Environmental Factors for Kanban Technique 1

- The plant is not excessively large.
- There is a high degree of commonality of components between various production lines and work cells.

Application of Kanban Technique 1

The common components master bins are centrally located within the plant. The individual production lines or work cells have subordinate kanban bins, and when they are low, they are taken to the master bins to be refilled. The master bins are triggered for replenishment. Delivery of replenishment is made to the centrally located rack.

Kanban Technique 2: Stockroom/Warehouse

This technique is applied when there is not enough room in the manufacturing area to handle the kanban lot sizes and there is a high degree of commonality throughout the factory.

Environmental Factors for Kanban Technique 2

- The OEM facility is extremely large.
- A high degree of commonality exists.
- Manufacturing floor space is highly limited.

Application of Kanban Technique 2

The master kanban containers are retained in the stockroom or warehouse. The subordinate bins are located at the point of use. The amount of line-side inventory has to be calculated to determine the amount of inventory at each location as well as the master containers.

Key Notes

1. *When numerous master bins are maintained for the same part number in different sections of a plant, limited supplier resources can create competition from the various areas in acquiring their materials with the supplier as their focal point. This is especially true when various sections of the plant are responsible for expediting their components directly from the supplier. Typically, it is best not to have more than one master kanban container per part number.*
2. *If a plant has more than one warehouse and the plant is extremely large, there may be no choice but to have more than one master kanban*

container. In this case, it is advisable to have a central point of communi-
cation to the supply base for replenishment. Multiple areas within the plant
can get fairly competitive in acquiring materials, which benefits no one.

Design Option 20: Deduct Points and Backflushing

The application of deduct points and backflushing is typically
applied to work cells and production lines that house hundreds of
components at the point of use and whose cycle time typically
exceeds several hours.

- *Deduct points* are intermediate-designated points in a work
  cell or production line, where the inventory consumed up
  to that point in the production process is subtracted from
  on-hand inventory and placed in a limbo account. There
  may be numerous deduct points within the work cell or
  production line.
- *Backflushing* is applied only at the end of the work cell or
  production line, and its action relieves the on-hand inventory from the last deduct point to its own location and
  decreases the limbo account of the previous deduct point
  action. The act of backflushing also increases the on-hand
  inventory of the completed item. Both the deduct point and
  backflushing are performed by entering the part number of
  the item being built and its quantity. This can also be performed by scanning a bar-coded manufacturing traveler, and
  then entering the quantity. The purpose of deduct points is
  to relieve the on-hand inventory count as soon as possible
  after it is applied to the item being produced, in order to
  simplify the cycle counting process and trigger replenishment of the single container option as soon as possible. (A
  computer monitors the total of on-hand inventory and on-
  order quantity, as compared to the kanban lot size). Backflushing eliminates the stockroom activity of picking parts to
  a specific work order, keying in the material that was
  applied to the work order, and then releasing the material to
  production. This way, the work cell or production line

builds what is triggered, utilizing the point-of-use material. At the end of the cell, simply scanning the bar-coded manu-facturing traveler and quantity of items built eliminates the non-value-added activity of keying into the computer all the part numbers and quantities that were used in producing the required items.

Kanban Technique 1: Deduct Points and Backflushing

Both deduct points and backflushing are applied.

Environmental Factors for Kanban Technique 1

- Stockroom kitting is not employed; material resides at the point of use.
- The work cell or production line cycle time is greater than two hours.
- Numerous components are used to manufacture the required items.
- The company dictates cycle counting.

Application of Kanban Technique 1

When an item being assembled reaches a deduct point and has its part number and quantity input into the system, the supporting part numbers that have been consumed and their respective quan-tities are deducted from the raw material on-hand inventory and placed in a limbo account. Each deduct point consists of support-ing part numbers that reside within its boundaries—from the last deduct point to the current deduct point. The spacing of the deduct points on the work cell or production line is usually based on time; for example, every 15 minutes worth of assembly time, there is a deduct point. Backflushing is positioned at the end of the work cell or production line, where the completed items are scanned or entered into the system along with the quantity, which subtracts the limbo account of raw materials placed there by deduct points and any other material consumed from the last deduct point to the backflushing location. The completed items are also incremented in the system, which is performed by the same backflushing transaction.

Key Notes

It would be almost impossible to cycle count a large work cell with many incomplete items without deduct points. Deduct points also provide immediate triggers for single container options. The advantages of eliminating the stockroom kit pulls are immense, and deduct points with backflushing eliminate a great deal of non-value-added activity.

Kanban Technique 2: Backflushing

Apply backflushing only.

Environmental Factors for Kanban Technique 2

- Stockroom kitting is not employed; raw material resides at the point of use.
- Cycle time through work cell is rapid.

Application of Kanban Technique 2

Only backflushing is employed at the end of the work cell/production line.

Design Option 21: Minimum/Multiples

Kanban Technique 1: Minimum/Multiple

Apply minimums and multiples to the kanban lot size calculation.

Environmental Factors for Kanban Technique 1

- Long setup times exist in the shop.
- Suppliers dictate minimum buys and package quantity sizes.

Application of Kanban Technique 1

Minimums and multiples are applied only to those kanban container options where the kanban lot size calculation actually becomes the kanban order quantity. It therefore applies to the container options of single full, dual, and triple. Minimums are applied first to the kanban lot size calculation, and then to multiples.

Minimums

Minimums are used to override the kanban lot sizes that are calculated for the container options single full, dual, and triple, where required. With these container options, the kanban lot size becomes the kanban order quantity, when triggered, as opposed to the container options single discrete (one-for-one) and multiple container (standard quantity size of container).

For example, if a kanban lot size for the dual container is calculated to be 600 pieces, its kanban order quantity will be 600 pieces. If a machine in the shop has a setup-time issue, the shop may dictate a minimum order quantity for the item, such as 1,000 pieces for this particular part number (the rationale here is that larger run quantities means fewer setups, which provides more time to produce pieces). In this case, once the kanban lot size of 600 is calculated, it will be checked to see whether a minimum exists. Because there is a minimum order quantity of 1,000 pieces, the kanban lot size of 600 would be changed to 1,000. Suppliers, on certain items, can also specify a minimum-buy quantity, and the technique of elevating the calculated kanban lot size would apply.

Multiples

Multiples are used when multiple part fixtures are used in numerical control machines to minimize automatic tool change on each component. For example, a fixture holds 100 components. Once the basic kanban calculation formula is applied, the kanban lot size is first compared to the minimum to ensure it exceeds the minimum order quantity, and is then rounded up by the multiple (e.g., 100). For example, 85 pieces is calculated by the kanban lot size formula. There are no minimums, but a multiple of 100 exists. The kanban lot size of 85 pieces will then be increased to 100 pieces. This pertains to the kanban container options of single full, dual, and triple. This technique also applies to suppliers, such as distributors who sell standard box quantities. For example, integrated circuits may come in tubes with 25 pieces per tube. In this case, a kanban lot size of 995 would be rounded up to 1,000 pieces.

Key Notes

If minimums and multiples do not apply to your environment, they are not employed. In the environments where they are required, care must be taken to avoid the liberal application of the minimums and multiples, because they inflate inventory.

Conclusion

The distinction between one manufacturing environment and another is often significant, requiring different kanban techniques to meet the needs of the company. These environmental factors include:

- Breadth and scope of product offerings
- Customer expectations versus manufacturing and delivery capability
- Predictability of demand
- Consistency of demand
- Linearity of demand
- Degree of part commonality
- Quantity of part numbers
- Size and volume of components
- Cost of components
- Inventory accuracy
- Setup-time capability
- Supplier distance and capabilities
- Supplier's minimums and multiples
- Size of manufacturing plant
- Distance of supporting cells
- Space limitations
- Software capability

This partial list may seem intimidating but, in fact, is easy to deal with once you have the knowledge. In addition, kanban is the one lean-manufacturing technique that touches virtually every corner of the business, which includes:

- Materials
- Manufacturing
- Sales and marketing
- Accounting
- Supply base
- Purchasing
- IT group
- Shipping and receiving
- Quality
- Industrial engineering

The kanban system is literally the heart of the business, which requires a cross-functional team to identify the environmental factors of the business and then select the appropriate kanban techniques. The goal is not how fast one can throw together a kanban system but rather how effectively the kanban system will operate in meeting the needs of your environment.

Chapter 7 deals with an important element of the kanban system, which is the supply base.

SUPPLY BASE KANBAN INTEGRATION

P urchased material and services represent the lion's share of the cost of goods sold for many companies. It is an area not to be taken lightly, because the success of most companies' business depends on the strategies, techniques, and relationships that are forged with the supply base. The supply base must be in total harmony with the OEM, and this can typically come about through long-term relationships and a joint-replenishment system that serves the needs of all concerned. There are too many variables in the day-to-day business that are outside the control of the supply chain; however, the variables that are within the control of the supply chain need to be eliminated. This means that the kanban system put in place must immediately calculate kanban lot sizes when demand is projected to shift, that pull signals are communicated without fault, that projected anticipated demand is shared for planning purposes, and that the overall kanban system is totally void of non-value-added activities for all concerned. The variables that stem from outside a supply-chain control can then be reacted to more effectively, because the kanban system does not have to deal with its own self-generated variables in satisfying customer demand.

The intent of this chapter is to focus on how to integrate the supply base onto the kanban system to ensure that everyone is in sync with satisfying the needs of the customer.

Design Option 22: Consolidating the Supply Base

Many manufacturers have hundreds and even thousands of suppliers. This is the remnant of past strategies that looked for the lowest price by having many different suppliers bid on the same items. Having many different suppliers actually works against the OEM from both a cost and kanban system standpoint. By consolidating the supply base, you can actually reduce the overall cost of material purchased based upon the overall volume of goods purchased from a single supplier. Equally important are the kanban system's considerations.

Being on kanban with a supplier requires a lot of work both for OEMs and suppliers. There will be little interest on the part of the supplier if the OEM does little business with them. The interest of suppliers to be on kanban escalates in direct proportion to the amount of business they will receive. Consolidation of the supply base is the starting point in integrating suppliers into the OEM's kanban system.

Kanban Technique 1: Consolidate Commodity Items

Consolidate the supply base that offers standard off-the-shelf items. This consolidation encompasses such items as electronic components, hardware, gaskets, and wire.

Environmental Factors for Kanban Technique 1

- The plant has a significant quantity of commodity items.

Application of Kanban Technique 1

Consolidating suppliers who offer commercial off-the-shelf commodity items is typically not complex but must be approached in a thorough manner. The following questions should be answered before selecting suppliers.

- **Do they carry a full line of products?** This is a key concern, because you want only a few exceptionally good suppliers who carry the vast majority of what you purchase. The intent is to leverage as much business as possible to the fewest sources possible, gaining leverage in your purchases from the standpoint of pricing, service, and working relationship.
- **Are they financially sound?** There are numerous ways to check this out, and one must be diligent in obtaining this information on each potential supplier.

- **How well have they performed in the past, and do they have a good relationship with your company?** Only the top performers can be considered. Past performance should not be left to opinion but backed by data such as delivery on-time reports and quality reports. Opinions matter when it comes to how suppliers have worked with your company in developing new product or in helping to resolve unexpected shortage issues.
- **Are they progressive and open to new ideas?** This is demonstrated by suppliers' computer systems and the quality techniques they employ, both within their own operations and with their other customers.
- **Would they be willing to go onto kanban with your company?** You must first be in a position to be specific in regard to your company's expectations, such as suppliers carrying the lead-time quantity or electronically acquiring triggered and projected demand. A number of items will need to be discussed, such as the kind of kanban containers that will be employed, who will pay for the empty containers' transportation, what will the lead times be once they receive the triggered signal, and what is the acceptable measurable level of performance. Are they interested?

Once you have centered on a few good supplier candidates who are interested in being on kanban with your company, have them bid on your anticipated projected demand. Create a negotiation worksheet routine, which can be used for both off-the-shelf items and specialty items (such as machine parts or stamping parts). (See Figure 7-1.) This computerized *negotiation worksheet* will list the items you are sending out for bid by commodity code. Have the routine acquire the part numbers, description, anticipated demand for the coming year, and standard price. Have the program multiply the standard cost by the anticipated demand for each part number and provide a total at the bottom.

After you receive the bids, key in the bid price and have the system extend out the totals and provide a total at the bottom of the

Negotiation Worksheet

Supplier: ABC Company   12/03/2007

Part Number	Description	Commodity	Anticipated Demand	Standard Cost	Extended Standard Price	Bid Price	Extended Bid Price	Difference
125647	Housing	75	14,780	$10.00	$147,800.00	$ 8.00	$118,240.00	($29,560.00)
126578	Bevel	75	1,567	$20.00	$ 31,340.00	$19.00	$ 29,773.00	($ 1,567.00)
135637	Lever	75	6,350	$10.00	$ 63,500.00	$10.50	$ 66,675.00	$ 3,175.00*
Total					$242,640.00		$214,688.00	($27,952.00)

Figure 7-1. Negotiation worksheet routine report.

worksheet. Print out the report. Compare your extended standards to the extended bid prices. This is your worksheet to negotiate each line and the overall total.

This routine is run for each of the suppliers who are bidding. Select your suppliers and make your contract as discussed in chapter 8.

Key Notes

1. *If any individual bid price is too good to be true, more than likely there is a misunderstanding on what is being bid. Check with the supplier to ensure there is no misunderstanding.*
2. *The negotiation sheet is not sent out to the supplier but rather is your tool for the negotiation process.*

Kanban Technique 2: Consolidate Specialty Items

You want to consolidate specialty items (such as with machine shops, stamping houses, and injection molding facilities), but this process should be handled with great care.

Environmental Factors for Kanban Technique 2

• The plant has a significant quantity of specialty items.

Application of Kanban Technique 2

Without question, those who have been in the business long enough realize that this technique must be approached carefully for the following reasons:

• Special tooling, dies, and fixtures are involved. Who owns them? What may be usable in one shop may not be applicable to another, due to the differences in machines.
• Blueprints may not be accurate. It is amazing how often it is not discovered that the prints are inaccurate until a new supplier is contracted to make the parts. The new supplier makes the parts according to the print, the parts come in, and the people using them encounter problems. The root

cause? The print has been wrong since the day it was made, and the original supplier over the years learned exactly what the real requirements were. But the prints were never changed. This is a common problem.

The objective is to consolidate all the machining with a given supplier, all the stamping with another supplier, and so on. Switching suppliers in this arena is, by its very nature, a concern and must be handled by experienced people who know the specialty items and the existing shops intimately. The costs and benefit of consolidation must be ascertained prior to switching suppliers and should be done methodically. If the decision is made to proceed with consolidation, it should be handled one step at a time, part by part. Have the shop you are migrating prove, with hard tooling, that they can manufacture the part to a blueprint that clearly reflects what is required. It is also a good idea to carry safety stock prior to making the transition with each part. A high degree of sensitivity must be applied to the suppliers who will be losing the business.

Key Notes

If any supplier is hesitant about going onto kanban, it is best not to force the issue but rather find a supplier who is willing to accommodate customers. Based on experience, whenever reluctant suppliers go on kanban, it is a sure bet that they will opt out after much effort and time has been put into them. There are many progressive shops—find them and develop a long-term partnership.

Design Option 23: Supplier Projection

The supply base requires a projection of anticipated demand on a regular basis. The frequency of providing the forward projection is as often as your company plans its production. The supplier projection is to be used by the supplier for capacity planning and determining supplier lead-time quantity. (See Figure 7-2.) The supply base will deliver only when the supplier receives a triggered order. There are several approaches to developing the projected requirements, and each depends on the technique selected to calculate kanban lot sizes.

Kanban Technique 1: Synchronized Explosion™ Supplier Projection

Have a computer routine pick up the respective quantities and dates of when kanban is projected to trigger from MRP's Planned Order Release row, and then summarize them by quantity within weekly or monthly time buckets.

Environmental Factors for Kanban Technique 1
- Synchronized Explosion™ is being employed.

Application of Kanban Technique 1
Once the MRP has performed the Synchronized Explosion™ for Design Option 3, Technique 1, have a simple routine pick up the OEM's part number, description, manufacturer's part number, and the quantities in the Planned Order Release row of the MRP, as shown in Figure 7-2. This, of course, reflects what has already been triggered and is anticipated to be triggered. This one line per item report is given to the supplier.

Key Notes

This method is typically highly accurate from an anticipated trigger standpoint. However, the intent here is to provide only a projection of anticipated demand from which the supplier can plan capacity and calculate lead-time quantities. This projection is not to be used by the supplier to deliver material to the OEM. Only triggered demand authorizes supply from the supplier.

Kanban Technique 2: MRP Gross Requirements Supplier Projection

Have a computer routine pick up MRP gross requirements for each part number and summarize the demand within weekly or monthly time buckets. Bear in mind that the information being supplied is

Supplier Projection

Supplier: Advanced Supplies

11/02/2007

Part Number	Description	Manufacturer's Part Number	November				Dec All	Jan All	Feb All
			5	12	19	26			
324	Capacitor	CJAHAFNCARBLVINQAM	360	0	180	180	720	900	900
367	Capacitor	CJOAYQRSJHBXESAYVLE	90	90	180	0	360	360	270
368	Capacitor	AEMNEXCAELJENTANOG	300	0	300	0	600	900	900
499	Resistor	AAVURCIEMVILIOQEJUH	200	0	400	0	800	800	1,000
567	Resistor	AIUDGRECATPIRIONFAA	600	600	1,200	600	4,800	4,800	5,400
600	Resistor	AEJRCKYGRESATPNIECN	700	0	700	0	1,400	1,400	1,800

Figure 7-2. Supplier projections.

not intended to provide the actual quantity and time periods of demand being triggered but rather an idea of the anticipated demand levels. The anticipated demand levels are to be used by the supplier to determine capacity and lead-time quantities. The gross requirements provided can be used to determine average daily demand by increment of time (week, month) and can be used for both purposes. MRP, by way of the gross requirements, provides the best source of information for the environment described in this section.

Environmental Factors for Kanban Technique 2

- A single-level bill of material MRP explosion is used to calculate kanban lot sizes.

Application of Kanban Technique 2

After MRP has exploded, have a simple routine pick up the OEM's part number, description, manufacturer's part number, and the quantities in the Gross Requirements row of the MRP, as shown in Figure 7-2. This information should suffice in planning capacity and calculating lead-time quantities. This report is given to the supplier.

Kanban Technique 3: Average Daily Demand Projection

Have a computer routine pick up the part numbers and the anticipated average daily demand.

Environmental Factors for Kanban Technique 3

- Historical usage data is used to determine a new projected average daily demand.

Application of Kanban Technique 3

This approach uses Design Option 3, Technique 3, historical adjusted average daily demand. Create a simple routine to pick up the newly calculated average daily demand for each part number. The file will contain the part number, description, manufacturer's part number (if available), and projected average daily demand. This one line per item report is given to the supplier.

Design Option 24: Supplier Lead-Time Quantities

Regardless of the replenishment system employed, the longer the supplier lead time, the greater the inventory levels for both supplier and OEM. Long lead times cannot be tolerated from the supply base, just as the OEM's customers will not tolerate long lead times from the OEM. With kanban, the supplier must ship the replenishment within a short period of receiving the triggered signal and must do so consistently. For those suppliers still going through the improvement process, the application of lead-time quantities can benefit both the supplier (in retaining the business until further improvements are made) and the OEM (from not being injured by the supplier's long response time or inconsistencies in on-time deliveries).

Kanban Technique 1: Supplier Control

There is no interference with the supplier's method of operation.

Environmental Factors for Kanban Technique 1

- The supplier immediately responds to triggered signals and consistently delivers the requirements exactly as contracted.

Application of Kanban Technique 1

The supplier is a world-class performer and does not require any special terms in the contract affecting its method of operation.

Kanban Technique 2: Lead-Time Quantities

The supplier agrees to carry the lead-time quantity. The lead-time quantity is completed supplier product sitting on the supplier's shelf. The formula used to calculate the lead-time quantity is average daily demand multiplied by the supplier's lead time to make or acquire the item.

Environmental Factors for Kanban Technique 2

The supplier is required to carry the lead-time quantity per contract, if any of the following conditions exists:

- The length of the supplier's lead time is excessive. The supplier's lead time should be relatively short, equal to the time needed to receive the OEM signal for replenishment and a few days to manufacture or acquire and pack, plus standard transportation time.
- The supplier's delivery on-time record is less than +99 percent.
- The supplier's delivery of the full quantity ordered is less than +99 percent.

Application of Kanban Technique 2

When the total of on-hand and on-order quantity falls below the lead-time quantity due to consumption (triggered releases from the OEM), suppliers are to launch an order for replenishment within their shops or initiate a buy from their suppliers. The contract will state that, in the case of obsolescence, the OEM is responsible for the inventory maintained at the supplier. The OEM is also responsible for exceptionally slow-moving inventory on the supplier's shelf.

Key Notes

1. The supplier, in reality, is not typically carrying more inventory than would occur under an OEM employing an MRP system. For example, under MRP, a machine part with a 6-week lead time with a 100-per-week demand would have an OEM launch a single order to cover a 6-week quantity and request that 100 per week be delivered. The supplier would run a 600-piece quantity (due to setup time) and deliver according to the 100-per-week release. The average inventory carried by the supplier would be half the lot size of 600 pieces, which would equal 300 pieces (6 weeks on-hand when made and zero at the end of 6 weeks). If the part is under kanban, the supplier would be asked to carry the lead-time quantity, which is

(6 week lead time) × (100 per week) = 600 pieces. When the 600 pieces are broken into, the supplier would run 600 pieces more, which will not be on the supplier's shelf for 6 weeks. The initial lead-time quantity on the shelf will go down from 600 pieces to zero on-hand in 6 weeks. The average inventory of the lead-time quantity is therefore half the lead-time quantity of 600 pieces, which is 300 pieces.

2. *Under MRP, both the supplier and OEM are carrying large amounts of inventory (MRP inventory turn ratios for MRP items for OEMs typically run between 3 and 12 turns). By the suppliers carrying the lead-time quantity on the shelf, they should be able to receive the signal, pack the item(s), and ship from their location to the OEM in 1 day. The replenishment lead time for the OEM is 1 day to send the signal, 1 day for the supplier to ship, plus transportation time, and receive and put-away time. The average inventory that the OEM must now carry will be half the purchasing replenishment lead time plus safety stock. If the purchasing replenishment lead time was 8 days with 1 day of safety stock, the average inventory would be (0.50) × (8 days) + 1 day safety stock = 5 manufacturing days = 1 week. Then 52 weeks in a year ÷ 1 week = 52 inventory turns per year. Under the MRP approach, both the OEM and supply base are penalized severely due to excessive supplier lead time. But under the lead-time quantity technique, the supplier carries the same amount of inventory as before, and the OEM's inventory turn ratio is accelerated tremendously.*

3. *The OEM must properly select items to be placed on kanban. If low-volume demand pattern items are placed on kanban with the suppliers, the end result will be slow-moving inventory sitting on the supplier's shelf that the OEM is responsible to acquire.*

Design Option 25: Supplier Interface

Once kanban has been triggered at the OEM, suppliers need to be given or sent a file communicating triggered demand and projected requirements. There are various methods of interfacing with the supply base and the technique selected is based on the environmental factors of the business, as covered in the following sections.

Kanban Technique 1: Manual Interface

The manual interface encompasses phone, fax, and supplier-scheduled delivery and pickup.

Environmental Factors for Kanban Technique 1
- Manual kanban card system is employed.
- Limited quantity of items is on kanban.

Application of Kanban Technique 1

For a small quantity of part numbers on kanban, this technique should suffice. Communication of triggered kanban for local suppliers who make pickups and deliveries is simply to give them the triggered kanban cards as well as a copy of the supplier projection report discussed earlier. For long-distance suppliers who do not perform pickups and deliveries, the triggered orders can be phoned in by the buyer, and the supplier projection report can be faxed.

Key Notes

Two problems can arise from the preceding technique: The first is lost kanban cards, and the second is that the intended individual at the supplier may never receive the fax. Someone else may have inadvertently picked it up.

Kanban Technique 2: Automated Electronic Connectivity

Automatically transmit files electronically in a ready-to-use format, using electronic data interchange (EDI), an extranet, an FTP server, and so on. Communicating the OEM's needs electronically is a highly effective technique for both local suppliers and suppliers located throughout the world.

Environmental Factors for Kanban Technique 2
- Automated kanban lot size calculation is employed.
- Automated triggering is employed.

- There are hundreds or thousands of part numbers on kanban.
- Suppliers are located in North America and throughout the world.

Application of Kanban Technique 2

The key objectives of this approach are to significantly reduce non-value-added activities and to mistake-proof the process of communicating triggered demand and projected requirements to the supply base. At the scheduled appointed time, connectivity is made and the files are transmitted to the supply base automatically.

Key Note

If the transmission of the file is not automated, the OEM's system should have an alert mechanism to advise whether a supplier has acquired the required files per the schedule dates and times.

Conclusion

The days of pitting one supplier against another for the lowest costs have given way to a more strategic approach. The telltale sign of the former days is a supplier list that numbers in the thousands. The objective, instead, is to minimize the number of suppliers, thus increasing the volume of business with the remaining suppliers, which translates into lower prices, lower operating costs, and partnerships that work seamlessly. For the supply base to be effective, suppliers require projections of anticipated demand from which they can plan their capacity requirements and determine lead-time quantities, where appropriate.

The interface with the supply base can be manual if you're dealing with only a handful of part numbers. But for companies who are dealing with hundreds or thousands of part numbers, with suppliers located throughout the world, the interface should ideally be electronic, employing an automated means of initiating connectivity and transmitting the data in a usable format for the supplier per the agreed-upon schedule. Automation removes the human ele-

ment from remembering to upload or download the required information. Electronically communicating in a ready-to-use format permits immediate use of the data by the supply base, which reduces
costs and time in reacting to the needs of the OEM.

In Chapter 8, we cover kanban implementation.

CHAPTER 8

KANBAN IMPLEMENTATION

K anban is an exceptional replenishment tool and, when designed and implemented correctly, actually appears to run itself. The shop floor and facility seems almost void of material, and people are not running around hand carrying parts. A kanban system that operates effectively is a reflection of the time and due diligence it took to properly design and implement it. Payment for not doing it right is due each day just like clockwork, in the form of requiring hot shipments from the suppliers, shutdown production lines, overtime, temporary workers, and overnight shipments to the customers. No other lean technique can create as much damage as an improperly designed or improperly implemented kanban system. But there is no need for this to occur. When the kanban system is designed for the environment and implemented correctly, a company can have a highly effective kanban system that pays for itself many times each year.

The typical steps to implementation are listed first and then covered in detail.

Step 1: Determine the (a) current state of the replenishment system, (b) recommended future state of a kanban system, and (c) rough-cut benefits of implementing a kanban system. Present findings and recommendations to executive level, obtain approval to proceed to the next step, and acquire an executive sponsor.

Step 2: Select a team leader.

Step 3: Form a cross-functional design and implementation team.

Step 4: Design your complete kanban system.

Step 5: Construct a detailed implementation milestone chart.

Step 6: Perform a detailed cost-benefit analysis.

Step 7: Acquire executive approval to implement.

Step 8: Put measurements into place.

Step 9: Initiate a manual pilot program of your system design.

Step 10: Program the required capabilities.

Step 11: Select your kanban candidates and determine your safety-stock settings.

Step 12: Implement company-owned distribution centers (if applicable).

Step 13: Implement manufacturing.

Step 14: Implement the supply base.

Step 1: Determine Current State and Future State (with Anticipated Benefits) and Present Findings

It is important that data be employed when assessing the current state. In addition, a preliminary design of the future state should be translated into rough-cut benefits, which help in seeking executive approval and support.

Current State

First, determine the current state of the replenishment system. For example:

- Current inventory turn ratio is 4.0; competition ratio is 10.0.
- Customer on-time delivery is 84 percent; competition on-time delivery is 98 percent. Root causes include:
  - Seventy percent of problem due to purchase part shortages. Out of 5,000 purchase part numbers, our current MRP procurement system generates 1,000 exception messages per week for realignments and cancellations and 800 messages to launch new purchase orders. System is far too nervous to be effective.
  - Thirty percent of the problem results from manufacturing component and assembly shortages. Major issues are the nervousness of MRP messages to cancel, realign, and launch orders. The company is unable to kit and

de-kit factory work orders fast enough per MRP's cancellation and launch recommendations.

• The company-owned distribution centers do not have a formal standard method in place to calculate what should be on the shelf. Each location has its own method.

Recommended Future State

Next, develop and recommend a future state with a rough-cut assessment of potential benefits of a kanban system. For example, a future state for your environment may include the implementation of a fully automated kanban system stemming from the company-owned distribution centers, directly to the specific production line responsible for replenishment, and to the specific supplier responsible for replenishment. This automated kanban system may have the following capabilities:

• **Automated distribution centers min–max (or kanban) calculations:** The system will automatically calculate each distribution centers' min–max (or kanban lot size), coupled with simulation capability to determine time period and quantity of projected triggered demand for each distribution center.

• **Automated master schedule:** The system will automatically acquire all of the distribution centers' projected triggered demand and automatically generate a manufacturing master production schedule.

• **Automated kanban calculations:** The system will automatically calculate kanban lot sizes for manufacturing and purchased items.

• **Automated sales order triggering:** When the total of the on-hand and on-order quantity falls below the kanban lot size (or the minimum, if min–max is used, instead), a sales order will automatically be triggered (e.g., from the company-owned distribution centers to the manufacturing plant). It will also calculate a due date.

- **Automated triggering:** Each production line will have supporting material located at the point of use and a manufacturing queue screen reflecting the items that have been triggered. They will be prioritized by an availability ratio and will perform a material simulation to determine material availability. The status of material availability will appear on the manufacturing queue screen. If a shortage exists, that information will appear on the manufacturing queue screen or buyer's screen for expediting.
- **Purchasing procurement:** All triggered items will automatically have a purchase order number assigned and be available for supplier download on the Extranet.
- **Distribution centers' excess inventory screen:** This screen will reflect the excess inventory of each distribution center and the distribution centers that can make use of that inventory.
- **Measurements:** A full complement of measurements will be in place.

Rough-Cut Benefits

The rough-cut benefits of implementing a kanban system include a potential inventory reduction of $9.3 million at the distribution centers. In addition, on-time delivery to customers is expected to go from 84 percent to 95 percent within the first three months of implementation.

For example, the rough-cut benefits may state that the distribution centers are carrying 13 weeks of inventory equating to $13,500,000. Their replenishment lead time to acquire supply from the manufacturing plant and place at the point of use is 2 weeks maximum (manufacturing plants ship once a week to consolidate; transportation and put-away lead time is 1 week). If the distribution centers were to carry 2 weeks of inventory for replenishment lead time, with 3 weeks of safety stock, their average inventory carried should equal (0.50) × (2-week lead time) + (3-week safety stock) = 4 weeks of inventory. This equates to a *potential* decrease of inventory carried of 9 weeks, equating to a $9.3 million reduction of inventory ($13,500,000 currently carried ÷ 13 weeks = $1,038,461 of inventory used per week × 4 weeks = $4,153,846 of inventory required, subtracted from current inventory at distribution of $13,500,000).

A rough-cut estimate of in-house inventory can be estimated in the same fashion. It is crucial to have the controller verify the math and concur with the logic prior to making the presentation. (If your demand patterns are very smooth and you are confident of the degree of safety stock and that the majority of part numbers are candidates for kanban, the preceding inventory reduction analysis may be applicable. If there is any uncertainty as to the percentage of part numbers that can be placed on kanban or the degree of safety stock required, you may combine this step with Step 11. This step determines the kanban candidates and the anticipated inventory reduction on a part number-by-part number basis.) Again, it is vital that the controller be involved to ensure there is agreement on the figures used and on the benefit calculation methodology employed for your environment. First and foremost, you want the assessment to be accurate. Second, during the presentation, the executive team will be looking to the controller to concur or disagree with stated benefits. The controller can provide invaluable insight, such as taking into consideration slow-moving and obsolete inventory when determining anticipated inventory reduction. Involving the controller benefits everyone.

Obtain executive approval to proceed to Step 2 and try to obtain an executive sponsor. An executive sponsor is recommended because resources will be required to perform the analysis, and having a sponsor signifies executive approval to proceed with the project to the company as a whole.

Step 2: Select a Team Leader

The team leader will, along with the executive sponsor, be responsible for the selection of team members. The team leader ideally should be someone who is highly respected, detailed-oriented, and organized, someone who understands the company's products and way of doing business and has a technical understanding of logistics, materials, and production. Most importantly, the individual should be skilled at leading others.

Step 3: Form a Cross-Functional Design and Implementation Team

Team members must be highly versed in their area of expertise, which will represent the sales, marketing, production, accounts payable, materials, production control, purchasing, IT, logistics, and accounting departments. Technical areas of expertise are key, but so is knowing the company—all of the company—intimately: its history; people; in-depth product knowledge; customer buying patterns; bill of materials structures; and quality of the data in the computer. This knowledge needs a *historian* who has many years with the company, is well respected, and can quickly point out those areas of concern that individuals with the technical expertise may not know about. Often, historians are the toughest members of the group to convince to adopt new methodologies, but there are several benefits that come from this:

- Often, excellent points come to the table from the historian, points that team members who have only technical backgrounds or short-term experience with the company may not be aware of. These points must be assessed completely to ensure that everything has been taken into consideration.
- The historian often voices the undercurrent of prevailing thought of other long-time, respected employees, and these thoughts must be addressed openly during the design process. Whether or not something is technically correct determines if and how it is applied. If what is being recommended is not technically correct, the person who is objecting should be able to state precisely why it is not technically correct.
- Making the historian part of the design process means that an important part of the company community will be heard and represented. When the design team as a whole agrees

to each step of the design process, a good part of the company is also agreeing. This greatly enhances the design and minimizes implementation issues upfront.

Ideally, the team can be devoted full time to the design and implementation. If that is not possible, the team must have scheduled times, and all members must attend each and every meeting.

Step 4: Design Your Complete Kanban System

Design is a lot of hard work, but it can actually be fun. Imagine creating your own replenishment system from scratch with the best of the best of the company.

Each kanban design option should be covered in the order presented in this text, and then discussed. The environmental factors of your environment should be identified and the associated technique considered to ensure that it meets your needs. Speed is not what is important here; you're looking for an in-depth assessment and selection of the specific techniques that will become part of your overall kanban system. Take time to gather the facts, and then obtain the consensus of every team member.

Once each technique is agreed upon, the details of its selection and how it will function will be written up in narrative form, explaining exactly how the selected technique will work. If it involves the computer routine, a step-by-step logic sequence will need to be spelled out, detailing the fields and files and calculation methodologies with examples. This information will be disseminated to each team member after the meeting.

The write-ups are read prior to the next meeting as the first order of business. If the write-up has an issue, it is discussed again, agreed to, modified, and presented again at the next meeting for approval. Once it is approved, it is placed in the kanban system binder. Each design option will go through this design process until all have been approved and recorded. If there are some unique areas that need to be covered, they will be added to the existing kanban design options and handled in the same manner. This process has the benefit of everyone knowing the details of the system being designed and what it would take from their standpoint to implement the system.

Step 5: Construct a Detailed Implementation Milestone Chart

The detailed implementation milestone chart reflects:

- Each task required to implement the kanban system
- The person responsible for each task
- The start and end date of each task

Performing the design and completing the detailed implementation milestone chart put everyone in alignment as to what needs to be done and the time that it will take to put the system in place. This information is used in Step 6.

Step 6: Perform a Detailed Cost-Benefit Analysis

Once the detailed implementation milestone chart has been created, it is time to perform a cost-benefit analysis. At this point, everyone is in agreement on the design of the kanban system and feels comfortable that it can be technically accomplished. Also, everyone has an idea of their roles and responsibilities, the tasks that are to be completed, and an estimated amount of time for each task. In addition, thought has been given to what may need to be procured, such as containers, racks, and any other supporting items. The team is ready to perform a cost-benefit analysis as follows:

Cost

Cost should include the following where appropriate:

- Containers
- Racking
- Computer monitors
- Bar code label machines

- Purchased software (for example, Extranet, EDI)
- Kanban card stock and printers
- Scanners
- Travel costs (distribution personnel)
- Training
- Outside consulting, if required

Benefits (tangible)

Tangible benefits should include the following, where appropriate:

- Customer on-time delivery improvements
- Inventory reduction
- Shipping cost savings (for example, alternative DC shipments and supplier overnight shipments)
- Shopfloor overtime savings
- Supplier reduction in premiums for rush orders
- Minimization of future obsolescence

Benefits (intangible)

Intangible benefits should include the following, where appropriate:

- Increased sales due to availability
- Higher customer satisfaction
- Growth as a result of being highly competitive
- Improved company morale

The company controller should verify the method of arriving at the benefits.

Key Notes

1. *An important ingredient in the benefits is the anticipated inventory reduction. A rough-cut methodology of determining inventory reduction was demonstrated under Step 1, and it may be applied if the demand patterns of your business are fairly smooth, where upon you know that the majority of part numbers can go onto kanban and you have a good*

estimate of the degree of required safety stock. If this is not the case, Step 11 should be looked at and employed for determining benefits for both Steps 1 and 6.

2. *All team members and the controller should be in alignment with costs and benefits before proceeding to Step 7.*

Step 7: Acquire Executive Approval to Implement

It is important that the team as a whole participate in the presentation to the executive staff. The team will present the:

- Current state
- Future state; the proposed system should be presented in summary format
- Anticipated costs and benefits

The presentation should be in a brief overview format, and the presenter should be prepared to go into detail, if requested. Once approval is given, the executive should make an announcement to the company that it plans to implement kanban and give the reason for action.

Step 8: Put Measurements in Place

It is vital to put measurements into place prior to implementation. Putting these measurements into place prior to implementation will serve as a baseline from which to judge the success of the implementation and to make modifications or adjustments to the kanban system. If measurements are not put into place, the system's success or need for modifications or adjustments will be left up to opinion (and not fact). There are three main areas to measure—distribution centers, manufacturing plant, and suppliers, as reflected in the following sections.

Distribution Centers

The following measurements need to be put into place for each distribution center and plotted on charts. This process must be initiated at least several months prior to implementation to gain enough history.

- **Inventory dollars on hand:** This is a simple chart, plotting the actual month-ending inventory. Drawn on this chart is the anticipated decrease of inventory.
- **Line item fill rate:** This measurement keeps track of the total number of line items of sales orders that were filled complete versus those line items that could not be filled complete due to shortages. The anticipated increase in fill rates is indicated on this chart.
- **Sales order fill rate:** This keeps track of the percentage of sales orders that were filled compete versus those that encountered a shortage. The anticipated increase in fill rates is indicated on this chart.
- **Missed sales opportunity:** Each time a request for an unavailable item was made by a customer and a sale was lost, track part number, description, quantity, sales price, and the extended lost sales in dollars. Add the extended dollars of lost sales by month. During implementation, details need to be studied to determine root causes, which should then be rectified. The anticipated decline in missed sales opportunities is indicated on this chart.
- **Obsolete and slow-moving inventory:** This measures the obsolete and slow-moving inventory. How inventory is defined as obsolete or slow moving is up to company policy. To measure obsolete and slow-moving inventory, use a calculation routine called Surplus Reserve Calculation Report. Typically, this can be acquired from your accounting department.

Key Notes

1. *It is important to chart individual locations as well as the aggregate. Just charting aggregate can mask specific issues occurring at one or more distribution centers.*

2. *Charting anticipated improvements is just as important as charting his-torical and current position. If the anticipated benefits do not occur as projected, the system must be checked immediately. For example, if inventory is decreasing more than expected and fill rates are lower than expected, ensure that the agreed-upon safety stock was put into the system. These charts also serve as information tools for diagnosing symptoms.*

Manufacturing

The following measurements need to be put into place for each manufacturing site and from an aggregate standpoint and plotted on charts. This must be initiated at least several months prior to imple-mentation to gain enough history.

- **Overtime:** Track and chart the overtime hours expended by each department and the plant as a whole monthly. Indicate on this chart the anticipated decrease of overtime.
- **Manufactured parts inventory levels:** For items that are manufactured or assembled in the plant, chart the monthly ending dollar inventory. Indicate the anticipated decrease of inventory on this chart.
- **Direct and indirect staffing:** Track and chart the staffing levels, broken down by direct and indirect monthly by department and for the plant as a whole. You want to ensure that no increases in staffing have occurred.
- **Line item fill rate:** This measurement keeps track of the percentage of total number of line items of distribution orders that were filled complete versus those line items that could not be filled complete due to shortages. Indicate the anticipated increase in fill rates on this chart.
- **Sales order fill rate:** This keeps track of the percentage of distribution orders that were filled compete versus those that encountered a shortage. Indicate on this chart the antici-pated increase in fill rates.

Suppliers

The following measurements need to be put into place several months prior to implementing the supply base.

- **Inventory on hand by supplier number:** Track the in-house on-hand supplier inventory by supplier number and in aggregate for all suppliers implemented. This is charted monthly. The anticipated decrease of inventory is drawn on the individual supplier chart.
- **Supplier performance levels:** This is a vital measurement. The measurement should measure supplier performance, with one number per supplier. What is measured is on-time delivery, ordered-full quantity received, and quality. Here is an example:

    Supplier M:

    100 items received month of November

    90 of 100 items received on time = 0.90

    80 of 100 items received full quantity ordered = 0.80

    92 of 100 items received with no quality issues = 0.92

    Supplier M's rating for the month of November = 66%

    $0.90 \times 0.80 \times 0.92 = 0.66$ (rounded) $\times 100 = 66\%$

What this means is that Supplier M can be counted on only 66 percent of the time not to stock you out. Have the computer system determine the supplier performance level and produce a supplier performance report monthly for kanban items. (See Figure 8-1.) This report should also produce a *detailed report* that reflects by supplier, by month, each receipt that took place. This includes the part number, purchase order number, quantity triggered, quantity received, due date, date received, and whether that receipt had a quality issue. It should show the decimal rating at the summation of the report, by category (items received on time, received full-order quantity, and quality).

Keep in mind that one overall measurement can also gauge the effectiveness of the supply base that is on kanban as a whole. This is accomplished by taking the individual supplier data that was

Supplier Performance Report					12/03/2007
Overall Supplier Rating					
Supplier	June	July	August	September	October	November
G	97%	97%	96%	97%	97%	98%
J	98%	99%	99%	92%	80%	69%
K	97%	97%	98%	96%	97%	97%
M	62%	65%	65%	58%	64%	66%
P	99%	99%	98%	99%	97%	99%

Figure 8-1. Supplier performance report.

demonstrated for Supplier M, by monthly time period, by each cat-egory (items received on time, received full-order quantity, and quality), for all the suppliers added together, and then calculating the rating. As an example, determine the total items received for the month that occurred for all suppliers versus the total that was received on time, and then compute the overall on-time decimal. Do this for each of the categories, and then determine the overall supply base rating by multiplying the decimals of the three cate-gories, and then multiplying the result by 100. At a glance, you have a very telling chart.

Key Notes

1. For the supplier rating report to be accurate, receipts must be processed through receiving and inspection (if required) the day they arrive at the back door.

2. The supplier performance report is absolutely vital. We can see in Figure 8-1 that we are starting to encounter an issue with Supplier J whose per-formance is eroding. The supplier was performing well but may be run-ning into financial problems or be under new management. In either case, the trend is quite clear: There is an issue that needs immediate attention. We can also see that Supplier M has had an on-going issue. You may wish to have this supplier carry the lead-time quantity until performance improves. If the supplier should have been carrying the lead-time quan-

tity, it appears as if it is not complying. The supplier may need your help, or some other type of action may have to be taken.

3. The purchasing contract should refer to the purchasing performance rating methodology reflected in Figure 8-1 as to how the level of performance will be measured. The contract will also state the minimum acceptable performance rating. In addition, each supplier should get a monthly scorecard reflecting its rating.

4. If any individual supplier's on-hand inventory begins to grow, check the minimum settings. They may have been applied too liberally.

Step 9: Initiate a Manual Pilot Program of Your Design

A *pilot program* is a limited manual implementation of your newly designed kanban system. The pilot program provides insight as to the soundness of the design of the kanban system. When applying the pilot to specific suppliers, select components that are off-the-shelf commodity items that can be readily obtained, if required. In other words, do not use the pilot for critical components until the pilot program has thoroughly proven itself. This is the time to make adjustments to the design before programming the required capabilities.

Step 10: Program the Required Capabilities

Ideally, a test box will be put into place where a copy of your new programs can be tested without affecting the current live system. Each routine, one by one, will be programmed, tested, retested, and approved by the users. If you have not located a number of programming bugs when testing, you probably have not tested the program thoroughly enough. Write a test procedure, knowing exactly what should occur ahead of time and put the data in place, engage the routine, and see whether the routine comes up with the correct output. Just playing with a routine once it is programmed will not suffice as a test. It is a good idea to have the key users of the system participate and sign off on the program. It is not unusual for the users to request modifications during testing, even though they may or may not have participated in the design. Many people cannot visualize the design or judge its merits until they are actually sitting down and working with the program. Some degree of change request is normal and should be accommodated if it makes sense. Put the extra time in your implementation milestone chart for these modifications to occur. Also, if there are any changes, the system write-up (being used to program) should be modified to reflect the changes.

Once the routines have been tested, have the users write the procedures for the routine. These procedures are vital because they deal with the timing and coordination of everyone on how to operate the system and how to handle exceptions. Team members need to sign off on the system write-up, procedures, and the routines. Keep system write-ups and procedures in a binder, maintaining and updating them as required. This binder is also used for new employee reference and training.

Step 11: Select Your Kanban Candidates and Determine Your Safety-Stock Settings

Not all part numbers can or should be placed on kanban. Examples include a sole-source supplier not wanting to participate on kanban, part numbers with quality issues, and an item that is being phased out. The most prevalent reason certain part numbers cannot be placed onto kanban is erratic demand patterns, even though a company has load-smoothed to the best of its ability. Erratic demand patterns create stockouts, and the only way to compensate is to apply safety stock. However, too much safety stock will inflate inventory levels and degrade the credibility of the triggering process, because it is known throughout that there is typically excess material. This leads to the question of "What do you really need?" and gives rise to the need for hot lists. A kanban candidate with the right degree of safety stock will typically not raise inventory beyond the pre-kanban level. The pre-kanban inventory level (for example, currently on MRP) is a good indicator as to whether an item is a good kanban candidate, when it is compared to the anticipated average inventory level if it were to be placed onto kanban. Designed and implemented correctly, the kanban system typically carries 30 to 65 percent less inventory than the typical results of an MRP system. Those part numbers with capability to reduce inventory and or maintain the same pre-kanban inventory levels need to be identified as kanban candidates so that other attributes such as quality, lead time (which cannot be excessive), supplier past performance record, and willingness to go onto kanban can be confirmed prior to placing them onto kanban. A number of MRP items may, in some cases, have a lower inventory than if they were placed on kanban. In some cases, it is not surprising that MRP is more effective, for example, in a job shop or make-to-order environment, or for an infrequently sold item, because the demand is here today and gone tomorrow. If these types of items were to be placed onto kanban, they would be carrying a predetermined on-hand inventory consisting of an excessively large safety-stock setting, as opposed to MRP, which is designed to satisfy the specific requirement at the correct point in time. Carrying a predetermined quantity of inventory on hand, under kanban, of infrequently used items will result in an increase of inventory with a high potential for stockout and obsolescence. Make no mistake: MRP is a great planning tool, but is a poor execution tool. However, it has its place in handling infrequently used items, which by their nature are erratic in demand and not good kanban candidates.

Two simulation techniques are demonstrated in the following sections. Both simulate and emulate each part number as if it were on kanban at the point of use. Enough detail is provided so that the individual OEM can program his or her simulation. Two different simulation approaches are demonstrated.

- Approach 1 is used when one safety-stock setting is applied to all the part numbers. Based on that one safety-stock setting for all the part numbers, you can determine the kanban candidates, appropriate safety-stock setting, and anticipated average kanban inventory levels, as they compare to current inventory levels from an individual part number and aggregate standpoint.

- Approach 2 determines an individual safety-stock setting for each part number and from this you can determine the kanban candidates, the appropriate individual safety-stock setting for each part number, and the anticipated average kanban inventory levels as they compare to current inventory levels. An automated simulation routine is applied to all the part numbers for both approaches. Although a number of aspects of these simulations are similar to the simulation used for calculating and testing kanban lot sizes, they operate differently.

Approach 1: One Safety-Stock Setting Is Applied to All Part Numbers

There are two parts to this simulation. Part One generates summary information to determine the degree of safety stock required for your environment. Part Two applies your choice of safety-stock setting and generates the detailed information, such as part numbers, on which are candidates for kanban and the degree of inventory reduction that may take place with that specific safety-stock setting. These two parts are demonstrated as follows:

Part One

The first part of the program calculates kanban lot sizes for each part number based on the 25 days of demand using historical or MRP projected gross requirements. It begins by using zero safety stock to the kanban formula. The routine will then perform a simulation, emulating exactly what would occur at the point of use day by day. Consumption will occur each day, kanban will be triggered, and replenishment will arrive according to its replenishment lead time. There is a different simulation routine for each of the container options that you plan to employ (single discrete, single full, dual/triple, and multiple). (See Figures 8-2 through 8-5.) (*Programming note:* For Part One, the detailed simulation showing the kanban lot size being applied day by day is not made available for viewing; this is just demonstrating what is occurring in the background in making a demand pattern analysis summary.) Part One of this simulation is trying to determine how many of the part numbers will stock out (zero on hand with an unsatisfied demand) by using zero safety stock. The stats of how many part numbers were simulated versus how many failed will be summarized and posted on a demand pattern analysis summary, as reflected in Figure 8-6. Once the results have been posted, the routine will automatically recalculate the kanban lot sizes, this time applying 1 day of safety stock, then post the results again to the demand pattern analysis summary, then rerun again, applying 2 days of safety stock, and so on. From the summary of results reflected in Figure 8-6, we can see that with zero safety stock, we would encounter a 75 percent stock-out rate. With 1 day of safety stock, we encounter a 12 percent stockout rate, and with 2 to 8 days worth of safety stock, we would have a 3 percent stockout rate. This is measuring the effectiveness of applying safety stock to your specific environment. It is a reflection on how severe your demand patterns are and how effective each increment of safety stock would be in eliminating stockouts. As you can see, if you were to select 1 day's worth of safety stock, the four items that stocked out would not be considered for kanban. If you selected 2 days' worth of safety stock, the one item that stocked out would not be considered for kanban. It is evident that adding any more days' worth of safety stock beyond 2 days would not be prudent.

Program the first part of the simulation as follows:

Step 1: Create an ASCII flat file containing these fields of information: Part number, description, replenishment lead time, minimums, multiples, container option, unit cost, on-hand inventory (reflection of MRP effectiveness), and MRP gross requirements or historical demand for 25 individual days. This information is provided for all the part numbers being considered for kanban.

Step 2: Have the program calculate kanban lot sizes, applying the kanban formula reflected by first adding up the demand for all 25 days, and then dividing by 25 to equal the average daily demand.

Safety Stock Simulation

Part Number: 15-2352
Description: Lower Plate
Item Container Option: SD Single Discrete

File record: 8
Lead Time: 2
Average Daily Demand: 80

Safety Stock: 0
Minimum: 0
Multiple: 25

Test Kanban Lot Size: 175 **Containers: 1**

Simulation Try Number: 1

	Date	Demand	KB1 Ending	KB2 Ending	KB3 Ending	KB4 Ending	KB5 Ending	KB6 Ending	KB7 Ending	KB8 Ending	Trigger Due	Simul. Trigger	Ending On Hand
1	11/1/07	85	90	N/A	N/A	N/A	N/A	N/A	N/A	N/A	0	85	90
2	11/2/07	90	0	N/A	N/A	N/A	N/A	N/A	N/A	N/A	0	90	0
3	11/5/07	75	10	N/A	N/A	N/A	N/A	N/A	N/A	N/A	85	75	10
4	11/6/07	88	12	N/A	N/A	N/A	N/A	N/A	N/A	N/A	90	88	12
5	11/7/07	72	15	N/A	N/A	N/A	N/A	N/A	N/A	N/A	75	72	15
6	11/8/07	78	25	N/A	N/A	N/A	N/A	N/A	N/A	N/A	88	78	25
7	11/9/07	80	17	N/A	N/A	N/A	N/A	N/A	N/A	N/A	72	80	17
8	11/12/07	85	10	N/A	N/A	N/A	N/A	N/A	N/A	N/A	78	85	10
9	11/13/07	79	11	N/A	N/A	N/A	N/A	N/A	N/A	N/A	80	79	11
10	11/14/07	69	27	N/A	N/A	N/A	N/A	N/A	N/A	N/A	85	69	27
11	11/15/07	70	36	N/A	N/A	N/A	N/A	N/A	N/A	N/A	79	70	36
12	11/16/07	75	30	N/A	N/A	N/A	N/A	N/A	N/A	N/A	69	75	30
13	11/19/07	78	22	N/A	N/A	N/A	N/A	N/A	N/A	N/A	70	78	22
14	11/20/07	85	12	N/A	N/A	N/A	N/A	N/A	N/A	N/A	75	85	12
15	11/21/07	90	0	N/A	N/A	N/A	N/A	N/A	N/A	N/A	78	90	0
16	11/22/07	84	1	N/A	N/A	N/A	N/A	N/A	N/A	N/A	85	84	1

Figure 8-2. Single container discrete simulation.

Safety Stock Simulation

Part Number:	15-2352	File record:	8	Safety Stock:	0
Description:	Lower Plate	Lead Time:	2	Minimum:	0
Item Container Option:	SD Single Discrete	Average Daily Demand:	80	Multiple:	25

Test Kanban Lot Size: 175   **Containers: 1**

Simulation Try Number: 1

	Date	Demand	KB1 Ending	KB2 Ending	KB3 Ending	KB4 Ending	KB5 Ending	KB6 Ending	KB7 Ending	KB8 Ending	Trigger Due	Simul. Trigger	Ending On Hand
17	11/23/07	87	4	N/A	N/A	N/A	N/A	N/A	N/A	N/A	90	87	4
18	11/26/07	80	8	N/A	N/A	N/A	N/A	N/A	N/A	N/A	84	80	8
19	11/27/07	70	25	N/A	N/A	N/A	N/A	N/A	N/A	N/A	87	70	25
20	11/28/07	80	25	N/A	N/A	N/A	N/A	N/A	N/A	N/A	80	80	25
21	11/29/07	80	15	N/A	N/A	N/A	N/A	N/A	N/A	N/A	70	80	15
22	11/30/07	80	15	N/A	N/A	N/A	N/A	N/A	N/A	N/A	80	80	15
23	12/3/07	80	15	N/A	N/A	N/A	N/A	N/A	N/A	N/A	80	80	15
24	12/4/07	80	15	N/A	N/A	N/A	N/A	N/A	N/A	N/A	80	0	15
25	12/5/07	80	15	N/A	N/A	N/A	N/A	N/A	N/A	N/A	80	0	15

Highest on hand stock level 90 observed on MDay 1. Lowest on hand stock level 0 observed on MDay 1. Average on hand stock level 0 observed on MDay 2. Average on hand stock level 18. Final lot size 175

Part Number 15-2352 is a single container discrete. It calculated a kanban lot size of 175 pieces, so we begin the simulation with a full kanban lot size as being on hand. When 85 pieces are consumed on Day 1 (11/1/2007), that leaves 90 pieces in kanban container 1 (KB1). Because the total of on-hand and on-order pieces equals 90, as compared to the kanban lot size of 175-piece kanban lot size, the difference of 85 is triggered (Simulated Triggered) for replenishment. On Day 2 (11/2/2007), the demand was 90 pieces, taking the on-hand quantity down to zero pieces, with 85 left on order equaling 85 pieces. This, subtracted from the kanban lot size of 175 pieces, triggers a replenishment order for 90 pieces. On Day 3 (11/5/2007), 75 more pieces were consumed, which were taken from the receipt of 85 pieces that were received from being triggered on 11/1/2007, leaving 10 pieces on hand. This process continues all the way down through Day 25. If there is an unsatisfied demand (zero on hand with an unsatisfied demand), the simulation will stop for this part number and consider it a stockout. If it makes it all the way through Day 25, it has passed the simulation. **Note:** See ending on-hand balances on the right-hand side. The ending balance for each day will automatically be added up and divided by 25 to determine the average inventory for this part number.

Figure 8-2. *continued*

171

Safety Stock Simulation

Part Number: 15-2354
Description: Key
Item Container Option: SF Single Full

File record: 10
Lead Time: 2
Average Daily Demand: 444

Safety Stock: 0
Minimum: 0
Multiple: 0

Simulation Try Number: 1

Test Kanban Lot Size: 888

Containers: 1

	Date	Demand	KB1 Ending	KB2 Ending	KB3 Ending	KB4 Ending	KB5 Ending	KB6 Ending	KB7 Ending	KB8 Ending	Trigger Due	Simul. Trigger	Ending On Hand
1	11/1/07	400	488	N/A	N/A	N/A	N/A	N/A	N/A	N/A	0	888	488
2	11/2/07	376	112	N/A	N/A	N/A	N/A	N/A	N/A	N/A	0	0	112
3	11/5/07	425	575	N/A	N/A	N/A	N/A	N/A	N/A	N/A	888	888	575
4	11/6/07	467	108	N/A	N/A	N/A	N/A	N/A	N/A	N/A	0	0	108
5	11/7/07	455	541	N/A	N/A	N/A	N/A	N/A	N/A	N/A	888	888	541
6	11/8/07	390	151	N/A	N/A	N/A	N/A	N/A	N/A	N/A	0	0	151
7	11/9/07	444	595	N/A	N/A	N/A	N/A	N/A	N/A	N/A	888	888	595
8	11/12/07	410	185	N/A	N/A	N/A	N/A	N/A	N/A	N/A	0	0	185
9	11/13/07	430	643	N/A	N/A	N/A	N/A	N/A	N/A	N/A	888	888	643
10	11/14/07	500	143	N/A	N/A	N/A	N/A	N/A	N/A	N/A	0	0	143
11	11/15/07	490	541	N/A	N/A	N/A	N/A	N/A	N/A	N/A	888	888	541
12	11/16/07	420	121	N/A	N/A	N/A	N/A	N/A	N/A	N/A	0	0	121
13	11/19/07	440	569	N/A	N/A	N/A	N/A	N/A	N/A	N/A	888	888	569
14	11/20/07	430	139	N/A	N/A	N/A	N/A	N/A	N/A	N/A	0	0	139
15	11/21/07	367	660	N/A	N/A	N/A	N/A	N/A	N/A	N/A	888	888	660
16	11/22/07	390	270	N/A	N/A	N/A	N/A	N/A	N/A	N/A	0	0	270

Figure 8-3. Single container full simulation.

Safety Stock Simulation

Part Number: 15-2354
Description: Key
Item Container Option: SF Single Full

File record: 10
Lead Time: 2
Average Daily Demand: 444

Safety Stock: 0
Minimum: 0
Multiple: 0

Test Kanban Lot Size: 888

Simulation Try Number: 1

Containers: 1

	Date	Demand	KB1 Ending	KB2 Ending	KB3 Ending	KB4 Ending	KB5 Ending	KB6 Ending	KB7 Ending	KB8 Ending	Trigger Due	Simul. Trigger	Ending On Hand
17	11/23/07	460	698	N/A	N/A	N/A	N/A	N/A	N/A	N/A	888	888	698
18	11/26/07	468	230	N/A	N/A	N/A	N/A	N/A	N/A	N/A	0	0	230
19	11/27/07	420	698	N/A	N/A	N/A	N/A	N/A	N/A	N/A	888	888	698
20	11/28/07	470	228	N/A	N/A	N/A	N/A	N/A	N/A	N/A	0	0	228
21	11/29/07	460	656	N/A	N/A	N/A	N/A	N/A	N/A	N/A	888	888	656
22	11/30/07	489	167	N/A	N/A	N/A	N/A	N/A	N/A	N/A	0	0	167
23	12/3/07	500	555	N/A	N/A	N/A	N/A	N/A	N/A	N/A	888	888	555
24	12/4/07	510	45	N/A	N/A	N/A	N/A	N/A	N/A	N/A	0	0	45
25	12/5/07	468	465	N/A	N/A	N/A	N/A	N/A	N/A	N/A	888	888	465

Highest on hand stock level 698 observed on MDay 17. Lowest on hand stock level 45 observed on MDay 24. Average on hand stock level 383. Final lot size 888

Part Number 15-2354 is a single container full. It calculated a kanban lot size of 888 pieces, so we begin the simulation with a full kanban lot size as being on hand. When 400 pieces are consumed on Day 1 (11/1/2007), that leaves 488 pieces remaining in kanban container 1 (KB1) and triggers a replenishment order for the full kanban lot size of 888 pieces. On Day 2 (11/2/2007), 376 more pieces are consumed, leaving 112 pieces in kanban 1 (KB1). Because the total of 112 pieces on hand and 888 pieces on order (a total of 1,000) exceeds the kanban lot size of 888, no additional orders are launched. On Day 3 (11/5/2007), a consumption of 425 pieces occurs as well as a receipt of 888 pieces (which, based on its replenishment lead time, was triggered 11/1/2007), leaving an ending on-hand inventory of 575 pieces in KB1. This process continues all the way down through Day 25. If there is an unsatisfied demand (zero on hand with an unsatisfied demand), the simulation will stop for this part number and consider it a stockout. If it makes it all the way through Day 25, it has passed the simulation. **Note:** See ending on-hand balances on the right-hand side. The ending balance for each day will be added up and divided by 25 to determine the average inventory for this part number.

Figure 8-3. *continued*

173

Safety Stock Simulation

Part Number:	15-2362	File record:	18	Safety Stock:	0
Description:	Stud Plate	Lead Time:	2	Minimum:	2,333
Item Container Option:	DC Dual	Average Daily Demand:	551	Multiple:	50

Simulation Try Number: 1

Test Kanban Lot Size: 2,350 — Containers: 2

	Date	Demand	KB1 Ending	KB2 Ending	KB3 Ending	KB4 Ending	KB5 Ending	KB6 Ending	KB7 Ending	KB8 Ending	Trigger Due	Simul. Trigger	Ending On Hand
1	11/1/07	1,500	0	850	N/A	N/A	N/A	N/A	N/A	N/A	0	0	850
2	11/2/07	550	0	300	N/A	N/A	N/A	N/A	N/A	N/A	0	0	300
3	11/5/07	580	2,070	0	N/A	N/A	N/A	N/A	N/A	N/A	2,350	2,350	2,070
4	11/6/07	560	1,510	0	N/A	N/A	N/A	N/A	N/A	N/A	0	0	1,510
5	11/7/07	550	960	2,350	N/A	N/A	N/A	N/A	N/A	N/A	2,350	0	3,310
6	11/8/07	540	420	2,350	N/A	N/A	N/A	N/A	N/A	N/A	0	0	2,770
7	11/9/07	560	0	2,210	N/A	N/A	N/A	N/A	N/A	N/A	0	2,350	2,210
8	11/12/07	540	0	1,670	N/A	N/A	N/A	N/A	N/A	N/A	0	0	1,670
9	11/13/07	480	2,350	1,190	N/A	N/A	N/A	N/A	N/A	N/A	2,350	0	3,540
10	11/14/07	530	2,350	660	N/A	N/A	N/A	N/A	N/A	N/A	0	0	3,010
11	11/15/07	490	2,350	170	N/A	N/A	N/A	N/A	N/A	N/A	0	0	2,520
12	11/16/07	410	2,110	0	N/A	N/A	N/A	N/A	N/A	N/A	0	2,350	2,110
13	11/19/07	505	1,605	0	N/A	N/A	N/A	N/A	N/A	N/A	0	0	1,605
14	11/20/07	480	1,125	2,350	N/A	N/A	N/A	N/A	N/A	N/A	2,350	0	3,475
15	11/21/07	525	600	2,350	N/A	N/A	N/A	N/A	N/A	N/A	0	0	2,950
16	11/22/07	540	60	2,350	N/A	N/A	N/A	N/A	N/A	N/A	0	0	2,410

Figure 8-4. Dual container full simulation.

Safety Stock Simulation

Part Number: 15-2362
Description: Stud Plate
Item Container Option: DC Dual

File record: 18
Lead Time: 2
Average Daily Demand: 551

Safety Stock: 0
Minimum: 2,333
Multiple: 50

Containers: 2

Simulation Try Number: 1 **Test Kanban Lot Size: 2,350**

	Date	Demand	KB1 Ending	KB2 Ending	KB3 Ending	KB4 Ending	KB5 Ending	KB6 Ending	KB7 Ending	KB8 Ending	Trigger Due	Simul. Trigger	Ending On Hand
17	11/23/07	600	0	1,810	N/A	N/A	N/A	N/A	N/A	N/A	0	2,350	1,810
18	11/26/07	580	0	1,230	N/A	N/A	N/A	N/A	N/A	N/A	0	0	1,230
19	11/27/07	490	2,350	740	N/A	N/A	N/A	N/A	N/A	N/A	2,350	0	3,090
20	11/28/07	500	2,350	240	N/A	N/A	N/A	N/A	N/A	N/A	0	0	2,590
21	11/29/07	600	1,990	0	N/A	N/A	N/A	N/A	N/A	N/A	0	2,350	1,990
22	11/30/07	0	1,990	0	N/A	N/A	N/A	N/A	N/A	N/A	0	0	1,990
23	12/3/07	530	1,460	2,350	N/A	N/A	N/A	N/A	N/A	N/A	2,350	0	3,810
24	12/4/07	600	860	2,350	N/A	N/A	N/A	N/A	N/A	N/A	0	0	3,210
25	12/5/07	530	330	2,350	N/A	N/A	N/A	N/A	N/A	N/A	0	0	2,680

Highest on hand stock level 3810 observed on MDay 23. Lowest on hand stock level 300 observed on MDay 2. Average on hand stock level 2348. Final lot size 2350

Part Number 15-2362 is a dual container. The same program is applied to a triple container, because there are never more than two containers in house at any given time. It calculated a kanban lot size of 2,350 pieces, so we begin the simulation with KB1 already having triggered 2,350 pieces and due within replenishment lead time (11/5/2007), and KB2 with a full kanban lot size of 2,350 pieces. When 1,500 pieces are consumed on Day 1 (11/1/2007), that leaves 850 pieces remaining in kanban container 2 (KB2). The container must be emptied in order for it to be triggered. On Day 2 (11/2/2007), a consumption of 550 pieces occurs, leaving an ending on-hand inventory of 300 pieces in KB2. On Day 3 (11/5/2007), 580 pieces are consumed, which uses up the 300 pieces that were on hand, plus the balance is taken from the receipt that has occurred from KB1. During this process, KB2 was emptied and triggered. This process continues all the way down through Day 25. If there is an unsatisfied demand (zero on hand with an unsatisfied demand), the simulation will stop for this part number and consider it a stockout. If it makes it all the way through Day 25, it has passed the simulation. **Note:** See ending on-hand balances on the right-hand side. The ending balance for each day will be added up and divided by 25 to determine the average inventory for this part number.

Figure 8-4. continued

Safety Stock Simulation

Part Number: 15-2369
Description: Right Brace
Item Container Option: MC Multiple

File record: 25
Lead Time: 2
Average Daily Demand: 12,416

Safety Stock: 0
Minimum: 0
Multiple: 10,000

Test Kanban Lot Size: 30,000 Containers: 3

Simulation Try Number: 1

	Date	Demand	KB1 Ending	KB2 Ending	KB3 Ending	KB4 Ending	KB5 Ending	KB6 Ending	KB7 Ending	KB8 Ending	Trigger Due	Simul. Trigger	Ending On Hand
1	11/1/07	11,000	0	9,000	10,000	N/A	N/A	N/A	N/A	N/A	0	20,000	19,000
2	11/2/07	10,000	0	0	9,000	N/A	N/A	N/A	N/A	N/A	0	10,000	9,000
3	11/5/07	10,500	8,500	10,000	0	N/A	N/A	N/A	N/A	N/A	20,000	10,000	18,500
4	11/6/07	0	8,500	10,000	10,000	N/A	N/A	N/A	N/A	N/A	10,000	0	28,500
5	11/7/07	11,000	7,500	10,000	10,000	N/A	N/A	N/A	N/A	N/A	10,000	10,000	27,500
6	11/8/07	13,000	0	4,500	10,000	N/A	N/A	N/A	N/A	N/A	0	10,000	14,500
7	11/9/07	12,867	10,000	0	1,633	N/A	N/A	N/A	N/A	N/A	10,000	10,000	11,633
8	11/12/07	9,050	2,583	10,000	0	N/A	N/A	N/A	N/A	N/A	10,000	10,000	12,583
9	11/13/07	12,000	0	583	10,000	N/A	N/A	N/A	N/A	N/A	10,000	10,000	10,583
10	11/14/07	12,000	8,583	0	0	N/A	N/A	N/A	N/A	N/A	10,000	20,000	8,583
11	11/15/07	12,000	0	6,583	0	N/A	N/A	N/A	N/A	N/A	10,000	10,000	6,583
12	11/16/07	15,000	10,000	0	1,583	N/A	N/A	N/A	N/A	N/A	20,000	10,000	11,583
13	11/19/07	14,000	0	7,583	0	N/A	N/A	N/A	N/A	N/A	10,000	20,000	7,583
14	11/20/07	12,000	0	0	5,583	N/A	N/A	N/A	N/A	N/A	10,000	10,000	5,583
15	11/21/07	13,468	2,115	10,000	0	N/A	N/A	N/A	N/A	N/A	20,000	10,000	12,115
16	11/22/07	14,000	0	0	8,115	N/A	N/A	N/A	N/A	N/A	10,000	20,000	8,115

Figure 8-5. Multiple container.

Safety Stock Simulation

Part Number: 15-2369
Description: Right Brace
Item Container Option: MC Multiple

File record: 25
Lead Time: 2
Average Daily Demand: 12,416

Safety Stock: 0
Minimum: 0
Multiple: 10,000

Simulation Try Number: 1
Test Kanban Lot Size: 30,000 **Containers: 3**

	Date	Demand	KB1 Ending	KB2 Ending	KB3 Ending	KB4 Ending	KB5 Ending	KB6 Ending	KB7 Ending	KB8 Ending	Trigger Due	Simul. Trigger	Ending On Hand
17	11/23/07	16,000	2,115	0	0	N/A	N/A	N/A	N/A	N/A	10,000	10,000	2,115
18	11/26/07	15,000	0	0	7,115	N/A	N/A	N/A	N/A	N/A	20,000	20,000	7,115
19	11/27/07	14,500	2,615	0	0	N/A	N/A	N/A	N/A	N/A	10,000	10,000	2,615
20	11/28/07	15,000	0	0	7,615	N/A	N/A	N/A	N/A	N/A	20,000	20,000	7,615
21	11/29/07	14,000	3,615	0	0	N/A	N/A	N/A	N/A	N/A	10,000	10,000	3,615
22	11/30/07	12,000	0	1,615	10,000	N/A	N/A	N/A	N/A	N/A	20,000	20,000	11,615
23	12/3/07	15,000	6,615	0	0	N/A	N/A	N/A	N/A	N/A	10,000	10,000	6,615
24	12/4/07	13,000	0	3,615	0	N/A	N/A	N/A	N/A	N/A	20,000	20,000	3,615
25	12/5/07	14,000	9,615	0	0	N/A	N/A	N/A	N/A	N/A	20,000	20,000	9,615

Highest on hand stock level 28500 observed on MDay 4. Lowest on hand stock level 2115 observed on MDay 17. Average on hand stock level 10659. Final lot size 30000

Part Number 15-2369 is a multiple container. It calculated a kanban lot size of 30,000 pieces which, when divided by the standard container quantity of 10,000, gives us three containers (KB1–KB3). When 11,000 pieces are consumed on Day 1 (11/1/2007), KB1 is consumed in its entirety, initiating its trigger for 10,000 pieces. The balance of 1,000 pieces is taken from KB2, initiating its trigger (containers are triggered once consumption on it begins) for 10,000 pieces. On Day 2 (11/2/2007), a consumption of 10,000 pieces occurs, consuming in its entirety KB2 and drawing 1,000 pieces from KB3, initiating its trigger for 10,000 pieces. On Day 3 (11/5/2007), 10,500 pieces are consumed, which uses up all of KB3, takes the balance required from KB1, which was just received, initiating its trigger for 10,000 pieces. In addition, KB2 had a receipt of 10,000 pieces. This process continues all the way down through Day 25. If there is an unsatisfied demand (zero on hand with an unsatisfied demand), the simulation will stop for this part number and consider it a stockout. If it makes it all the way through Day 25, it has passed the simulation. **Note:** See ending on-hand balances on the right-hand side. The ending balance for each day is added up and divided by 25 to determine the average inventory for this part number.

Figure 8-5. continued

177

Demand Pattern Analysis			
Safety Stock Added	Part Numbers Assessed	Part Numbers Stocked Out	Percent Stocked Out
0	33	25	75.76%
1	33	4	12.12%
2	33	1	3.03%
3	33	1	3.03%
4	33	1	3.03%
5	33	1	3.03%
6	33	1	3.03%
7	33	1	3.03%
8	33	1	3.03%
9	33	0	0.00%
10	33	0	0.00%

Figure 8-6. Demand pattern analysis.

Step 3: Multiply the average daily demand by lead time plus zero day's safety stock to equal the kanban lot size and apply minimums and multiples, where applicable.

Step 4: Program the simulations as reflected in Figure 8-2 through 8-5. For all items that you test in this manner, assume that you have the full kanban lot size quantity on hand prior to starting Day 1, and that there is zero on order with the exception of the dual/triple container option, which begins with 1 container on hand and 1 already triggered.

Step 5: Have the program summarize the results (how many part numbers were tested versus how many stocked out) using zero safety stock, as seen on the first line of the demand pattern analysis report in Figure 8-6.

Step 6: Now have the program begin the process again, this time using 1 day of safety stock in calculating the kanban lot size, and then performing the simulation. Now have the program post the summary of results for using 1 day of safety stock, as seen in Figure 8-6. This process repeats itself according to the user's setting, which in this case was set to go up to 10 days worth of safety stock.

In viewing Figure 8-6, you would be prudent to set the safety-stock level at either 1 or 2 days, but the choice depends on what the average inventory levels will be for 1 day of safety stock, and then for 2 days of safety stock, and how those inventory levels differ from what you are currently carrying under MRP.

Part Two

The same ASCII flat file is applied. This program, however, requests that you input the safety-stock setting you are considering (for example, 1 day). Once input, the simulation will take place and provide the following:

- The simulation detail will be shown for all part numbers that have passed or failed the simulation, as shown in Figures 8-2 through 8-5. Note the Ending Inventory column on the right-hand side of the simulation. These quantities represent the ending inventory after each day of the simulation. They are added, and then divided by the number of days in the simulation to determine the average kanban inventory on hand for each part number. For each part number, this average inventory on hand will then be multiplied times the unit cost, and then be compared to the current on-hand inventory. (Current on-hand inventory represents the effectiveness of the current replenishment system, for example, MRP.)
- A detailed list of all the part numbers that passed the simulation with lower projected anticipated average inventory levels under kanban as compared to the current on-hand inventory will be generated. (See Figure 8-7.) Note at the bottom of column headed Current Dollars on Hand that, under MRP, these on-hand items represent $2.2 million dollars of inventory. Under the column Simulated Dollars On

Sorted by Dollar Difference

Passed Simulation With Lower Inventory

General Safety Stock Setting: 1

Part Number	Description	Unit Cost	Quantity On Hand	Current Dollars On Hand	Simulated Average Inventory	Simulated Dollars On Hand	Projected Inventory Change
15-2357	Left Jack	$0.58	3,000,123	$1,740,071.34	1,180,117	$684,467.86	($1,055,603.48)
15-2372	Lower Panel	$7.30	18,700	$136,510.00	10,765	$78,584.50	($57,925.50)
15-2370	Left Brace	$6.30	16,162	$101,820.60	10,640	$67,032.00	($34,788.60)
15-2369	Right Brace	$6.00	23,832	$142,992.00	20,659	$123,954.00	($19,038.00)
15-2375	Upper Base	$52.87	278	$14,697.86	23	$1,216.01	($13,481.85)
15-2376	Rear Panel	$45.32	350	$15,862.00	81	$3,670.92	($12,191.08)
15-2366	Wedge	$55.89	453	$25,318.17	267	$14,922.63	($10,395.54)
15-2374	Blade Arm	$33.76	198	$6,684.48	40	$1,350.40	($5,334.08)
15-2362	Stud Plate	$8.09	2,967	$24,003.03	2,348	$18,995.32	($5,007.71)
15-2364	Housing	$45.00	279	$12,555.00	205	$9,225.00	($3,330.00)
15-2377	Rotor Shaft	$5.50	476	$2,618.00	91	$500.50	($2,117.50)
15-2371	Wedge Clamp	$8.00	567	$4,536.00	313	$2,504.00	($2,032.00)
15-2359	Lower Joint with upper sleeve	$22.55	250	$5,637.50	195	$4,397.25	($1,240.25)
15-2361	Cinder Lever	$6.98	543	$3,790.14	474	$3,308.52	($481.62)
15-2363	Clamp	$6.00	458	$2,748.00	392	$2,352.00	($396.00)
15-2347	Jumper	$2.77	215	$595.55	114	$315.78	($279.77)
15-2365	Sleeve	$1.00	444	$444.00	205	$205.00	($239.00)
15-2373	Upper Panel	$4.40	57	$250.80	25	$110.00	($140.80)
15-2350	Jack	$7.90	66	$521.40	50	$395.00	($126.40)
15-2351	Plate Jack	$2.75	125	$343.75	83	$228.25	($115.50)
15-2352	Lower Plate	$1.00	200	$200.00	93	$93.00	($107.00)
15-2378	Front Panel	$4.58	789	$3,613.62	774	$3,544.92	($68.70)
15-2349	Splice	$0.05	3,200	$160.00	2,472	$123.60	($36.40)
321	Gear Assembly	$1.00	40	$40.00	14	$14.00	($26.00)
Grand Total				**$2,246,013.24**		**$1,021,510.46**	**($1,224,502.78)**

Hand, the average inventory if these items were placed on kanban should equal $1.0 million dollars. This is a $1.2 million reduction in inventory if we place these part numbers onto kanban. These are your kanban candidates.

- A detailed list of all the part numbers that passed the simulation with higher projected anticipated average inventory levels under kanban, as compared to the current on-hand quantity is generated. (See Figure 8-8.) It is the user's discretion whether these items are placed on kanban; nonetheless, it informs the user of the degree of inventory that would increase. Some of the increases in dollars could be very small, making a part a good candidate.
- A detailed list of all the part numbers that failed the simulation is generated. (See Figure 8-9.) These are not kanban candidates.

The user will then run the simulation again, this time with a safety-stock setting of 2 days. The results of these two simulations (1 day of safety stock versus 2 days) will be compared and assessed, and a determination of the appropriate safety-stock setting and kanban candidates will be made based on the results.

This technique is used to determine the appropriate safety-stock setting, determine kanban candidates, and determine what the average inventory levels should be for the kanban candidates as opposed to the current inventory levels operating under MRP or some other method. This tool is designed to be used as an ongoing way to set safety stock and to reassess current kanban items, as demand patterns tend to shift with time. The frequency of reassessment depends on the degree of change an environment experiences in time.

Key Notes

1. *Some OEMs are extremely large and have the total attention of their supply base, which is within a few miles of their facility, and they prefer to use one safety-stock setting for all their kanban part numbers. From experience it can be said that the superior method is to determine safety-stock setting for each individual part number based upon its own unique*

Passed Simulation With Higher Inventory

Sorted by Dollar Difference

General Safety Stock Setting: 1

Part Number	Description	Unit Cost	Quantity On Hand	Current Dollars On Hand	Simulated Average Inventory	Simulated Dollars On Hand	Projected Inventory Change
15-2368	Pin Rod	$8.99	895	$8,046.05	3,252	$29,235.48	$21,189.43
15-2354	Key	$3.50	250	$875.00	1,040	$3,640.00	$2,765.00
15-2356	Stud	$9.95	16,162	$1,194.00	342	$3,402.90	$2,208.90
15-2353	Rotor	$0.88	120	$700.48	1,175	$1,034.00	$333.52
15-2355	Needle	$1.00	796	$185.00	195	$195.00	$10.00
Grand Total				$11,000.53		$37,507.38	$26,506.85

Figure 8-8. Passed simulation with higher inventory: 1-day safety-stock setting.

Failed Simulation Non Kanban Candidates

Part Number	Description	Average Demand	Lead Time	Safety Stock	Minimum	Multiple	Kanban Lot Size	Period Failed
15-2348	Gear	79	2	1	0	0	237	2
15-2358	Upper Base	2,624	2	1	0	0	7,872	22
15-2360	Bearing Pin	87	2	1	0	0	261	2
15-2367	Plug	155	2	1	0	0	465	2

Figure 8-9. Failed the simulation: 1-day safety-stock setting.

demand patterns. Typically, the end result is that more part numbers will pass as kanban candidates and the average kanban inventory levels will be significantly lower. This is demonstrated in Approach 2, in the following section.

2. *Either historical usage or MRP's forward projection is used. The demand patterns in either case must be considered representative of the degree of variability that is expected to repeat. As a general rule, history repeats itself, but not always.*

3. *To employ MRP gross requirements, the master production schedule is used to drive the MRP explosion. Ensure that your particular MRP module does not go gross to net against the master production schedule, because on-hand inventory may have already been taken into consideration in its construction. If this is the case, make a copy of your MRP module and make the necessary modifications. The MRP main procedure should then be modified to reference the modified MRP. The referenced MRP will now be in production. The IT group thus retains the capability to refer back to the original MRP if the need arises. It is, of course, the responsibility of IT to determine the most effective means for their particular ERP/MRPII package.*

4. *This tool, like all other techniques covered in this book, needs to be tested rigorously to ensure that it will serve the needs of the environment. After testing, apply it to a pilot area manually, and study the results. If it meets your needs, program it and test it rigorously to ensure it functions as designed.*

5. *Safety stock required for late deliveries and other issues are added as required.*

Approach 2: Determine an Individual Safety-Stock Setting for Each Part Number

This technique uses the same ASCII flat file of information as Approach 1. The simulation utilizes the simulation format shown in Figures 8-2 through 8-5; however, it is performed differently. It will calculate the kanban lot sizes using zero safety stock, run the simulation, and if the simulation fails for any part number, the program will automatically increase the calculated kanban lot size by 10 percent (10 percent represents safety stock) and rerun the simulation.

This process will repeat itself up to 30 times (as an example) and will discontinue until either the kanban lot size passes the simulation or 30 attempts have failed. See Figure 8-10, which is a single full container option. In this figure, you can see that the average daily demand for part number 15-2353 is 463 pieces, multiplied by a lead time of 2 days, equaling a kanban lot size of 926 pieces. There are no minimums or multiples required for this example. As you can see from the simulation, a stockout occurred in Day 19 for 7 pieces. The simulation program will stop and then increase the preliminary kanban lot size of 926 by 10 percent (1.10 times 926) to equal a new kanban lot size of 1,019 pieces. As you can see from Figure 8-10, in the second attempt, beginning in the row labeled Simulation Try 2, the simulation begins again, this time testing the increased kanban lot size of 1,019 pieces. The kanban lot size of 1,019 pieces has passed the simulation. The program will then generate a Safety Stock Required, Not Rounded report. (See Figure 8-11.) This report shows the part number, description, unit cost, average daily demand, lead-time quantity, simulated kanban lot size, required safety stock, and expected safety-stock dollars. The lead-time quantity for part number 15-2353 (for example, 926 pieces) was calculated by taking the lead time (for example, 2 days), and then multiplying it by the average daily demand (for example 463). The difference between the lead-time quantity and the kanban lot size that passed the simulation (for example, 1,019) is the safety-stock quantity (for example, 1,019 kanban lot size less 926 pieces lead-time quantity), which, in the case of part number 15-2353, is 93 pieces. The safety stock of 93 pieces is then divided by the average daily demand (93-piece safety stock ÷ 463-piece average daily demand) to equal the safety-stock setting, which in this example is 0.2 days of safety stock. To recheck the calculation, apply the kanban lot size formula: (463-piece average daily demand) × (2-day lead time + 0.2-day safety stock) = 1,019 (rounded).

The simulation routine will then generate a listing of the part numbers that, in this case, passed the simulation with a lower average inventory than what is currently on hand. (See Figure 8-12.)

Safety Stock Simulation

Part Number: 15-2353
Description: Rotor
Item Container Option: SF Single Full

File record: 9
Lead Time: 2
Average Daily Demand: 463

Safety Stock: 0
Minimum: 0
Multiple: 0

Simulation Try Number: 1

Test Kanban Lot Size: 926 Containers: 1

	Date	Demand	KB1 Ending	KB2 Ending	KB3 Ending	KB4 Ending	KB5 Ending	KB6 Ending	KB7 Ending	KB8 Ending	Trigger Due	Simul. Trigger	Ending On Hand
1	11/1/07	222	704	N/A	N/A	N/A	N/A	N/A	N/A	N/A	0	926	704
2	11/2/07	350	354	N/A	N/A	N/A	N/A	N/A	N/A	N/A	0	0	354
3	11/5/07	400	880	N/A	N/A	N/A	N/A	N/A	N/A	N/A	926	926	880
4	11/6/07	500	380	N/A	N/A	N/A	N/A	N/A	N/A	N/A	0	0	380
5	11/7/07	460	846	N/A	N/A	N/A	N/A	N/A	N/A	N/A	926	926	846
6	11/8/07	468	378	N/A	N/A	N/A	N/A	N/A	N/A	N/A	0	0	378
7	11/9/07	440	864	N/A	N/A	N/A	N/A	N/A	N/A	N/A	926	926	864
8	11/12/07	350	514	N/A	N/A	N/A	N/A	N/A	N/A	N/A	0	0	514
9	11/13/07	430	1,010	N/A	N/A	N/A	N/A	N/A	N/A	N/A	926	0	1,010
10	11/14/07	450	560	N/A	N/A	N/A	N/A	N/A	N/A	N/A	0	926	560
11	11/15/07	460	100	N/A	N/A	N/A	N/A	N/A	N/A	N/A	0	0	100
12	11/16/07	450	576	N/A	N/A	N/A	N/A	N/A	N/A	N/A	926	926	576
13	11/19/07	380	196	N/A	N/A	N/A	N/A	N/A	N/A	N/A	0	0	196
14	11/20/07	500	622	N/A	N/A	N/A	N/A	N/A	N/A	N/A	926	926	622
15	11/21/07	525	97	N/A	N/A	N/A	N/A	N/A	N/A	N/A	0	0	97
16	11/22/07	460	563	N/A	N/A	N/A	N/A	N/A	N/A	N/A	926	926	563

Figure 8-10. Simulation failed kanban lot size increased, and then passes.

Safety Stock Simulation

Part Number: 15-2353
Description: Rotor
Item Container Option: SF Single Full

File record: 9
Lead Time: 2
Average Daily Demand: 463

Safety Stock: 0
Minimum: 0
Multiple: 0

	Date	Demand	KB1 Ending	KB2 Ending	KB3 Ending	KB4 Ending	KB5 Ending	KB6 Ending	KB7 Ending	KB8 Ending	Trigger Due	Simul. Trigger	Ending On Hand
Simulation Try Number: 1						**Test Kanban Lot Size: 926**						**Containers: 1**	
17	11/23/07	466	97	N/A	N/A	N/A	N/A	N/A	N/A	N/A	0	0	97
18	11/26/07	500	523	N/A	N/A	N/A	N/A	N/A	N/A	N/A	926	926	523
19	11/27/07	530	523	N/A	N/A	N/A	N/A	N/A	N/A	N/A	0	0	–7

Lot size failed on day 19 (shortage of 7), will raise lot size and try again.

	Date	Demand	KB1 Ending	KB2 Ending	KB3 Ending	KB4 Ending	KB5 Ending	KB6 Ending	KB7 Ending	KB8 Ending	Trigger Due	Simul. Trigger	Ending On Hand
Simulation Try Number: 2						**Test Kanban Lot Size: 1,019**						**Containers: 1**	
1	11/1/07	222	797	N/A	N/A	N/A	N/A	N/A	N/A	N/A	0	1,019	797
2	11/2/07	350	447	N/A	N/A	N/A	N/A	N/A	N/A	N/A	0	0	447
3	11/5/07	400	1,066	N/A	N/A	N/A	N/A	N/A	N/A	N/A	1,019	0	1,066
4	11/6/07	500	566	N/A	N/A	N/A	N/A	N/A	N/A	N/A	0	1,019	566
5	11/7/07	460	106	N/A	N/A	N/A	N/A	N/A	N/A	N/A	0	0	106
6	11/8/07	468	657	N/A	N/A	N/A	N/A	N/A	N/A	N/A	1,019	1,019	657
7	11/9/07	440	217	N/A	N/A	N/A	N/A	N/A	N/A	N/A	0	0	217
8	11/12/07	350	886	N/A	N/A	N/A	N/A	N/A	N/A	N/A	1,019	1,019	886
9	11/13/07	430	456	N/A	N/A	N/A	N/A	N/A	N/A	N/A	0	0	456
10	11/14/07	450	1,025	N/A	N/A	N/A	N/A	N/A	N/A	N/A	1,019	0	1,025
11	11/15/07	460	565	N/A	N/A	N/A	N/A	N/A	N/A	N/A	0	1,019	565

Figure 8-10. Simulation failed kanban lot size increased, and then passes (*continued*).

Safety Stock Simulation

Part Number: 15-2353
Description: Rotor
Item Container Option: SF Single Full

File record: 9
Lead Time: 2
Average Daily Demand: 463

Safety Stock: 0
Minimum: 0
Multiple: 0

Containers: 1

Test Kanban Lot Size: 1,019

Simulation Try Number: 2

	Date	Demand	KB1 Ending	KB2 Ending	KB3 Ending	KB4 Ending	KB5 Ending	KB6 Ending	KB7 Ending	KB8 Ending	Trigger Due	Simul. Trigger	Ending On Hand
12	11/16/07	450	115	N/A	N/A	N/A	N/A	N/A	N/A	N/A	0	0	115
13	11/19/07	380	754	N/A	N/A	N/A	N/A	N/A	N/A	N/A	1,019	1,019	754
14	11/20/07	500	254	N/A	N/A	N/A	N/A	N/A	N/A	N/A	0	0	254
15	11/21/07	525	748	N/A	N/A	N/A	N/A	N/A	N/A	N/A	1,019	1,019	748
16	11/22/07	460	288	N/A	N/A	N/A	N/A	N/A	N/A	N/A	0	0	288
17	11/23/07	466	841	N/A	N/A	N/A	N/A	N/A	N/A	N/A	1,019	1,019	841
18	11/26/07	500	341	N/A	N/A	N/A	N/A	N/A	N/A	N/A	0	0	341
19	11/27/07	530	830	N/A	N/A	N/A	N/A	N/A	N/A	N/A	1,019	1,019	830
20	11/28/07	540	290	N/A	N/A	N/A	N/A	N/A	N/A	N/A	0	0	290
21	11/29/07	550	759	N/A	N/A	N/A	N/A	N/A	N/A	N/A	1,019	1,019	759
22	11/30/07	540	219	N/A	N/A	N/A	N/A	N/A	N/A	N/A	0	0	219
23	12/3/07	540	698	N/A	N/A	N/A	N/A	N/A	N/A	N/A	1,019	1,019	698
24	12/4/07	489	209	N/A	N/A	N/A	N/A	N/A	N/A	N/A	0	0	209
25	12/5/07	560	668	N/A	N/A	N/A	N/A	N/A	N/A	N/A	1,019	1,019	668

Highest on hand stock level 1066 observed on MDay 2. Lowest on hand stock level 106 observed on MDay 3. Average on hand stock level 552. Final lot size 1019

Figure 8-10. Simulation failed kanban lot size increased, and then passes (*continued*).

Safety Stock Required—Not Rounded

Passed Simulation

Part Number	Description	Unit Cost	Average Daily Demand	Lead Time Qty.	Simulated Kanban Lot Size	Required Safety Stock	Expected Safety Stock Dollars
15-2346	Left Holder	1.00	43	86	105	0.4	$17.20
15-2347	Jumper	2.77	112	224	328	0.9	$279.22
15-2348	Gear	4.50	79	158	279	1.5	$533.25
15-2349	Splice	0.05	2,342	4,684	6,857	0.9	$105.39
15-2350	Jack	7.90	48	96	142	1.0	$379.20
15-2351	Plate Jack	2.75	80	160	176	0.2	$44.00
15-2352	Lower Plate	1.00	80	175	175	0.0	$0.00
15-2353	Rotor	0.88	463	926	1,019	0.2	$81.49
15-2354	Key	3.50	444	888	888	0.0	$0.00
15-2355	Needle	1.00	80	160	176	0.2	$16.00
15-2356	Stud	9.95	144	288	349	0.4	$573.12
15-2357	Left Jack	0.58	450,194	1,000,000	1,000,000	0.0	$0.00
15-2358	Upper Base	4.50	2,624	5,248	29,180	9.1	$107,452.80
15-2359	Lower Joint with upper sleeve	22.55	80	160	176	0.2	$360.80
15-2360	Bearing Pin	1.00	87	174	338	1.9	$165.30
15-2361	Cinder Lever	6.98	209	418	506	0.4	$583.53
15-2362	Stud Plate	8.09	551	2,350	2,350	0.0	$0.00
15-2363	Clamp	6.00	168	336	407	0.4	$403.20
15-2364	Housing	45.00	80	160	176	0.2	$720.00
15-2365	Sleeve	1.00	80	160	176	0.2	$16.00
15-2366	Wedge	55.89	106	212	256	0.4	$2,369.74
15-2367	Plug	3.00	155	310	549	1.5	$697.50
15-2368	Pin Rod	8.99	1,248	2,496	2,746	0.2	$2,243.90
15-2369	Right Brace	6.00	12,416	30,000	30,000	0.0	$0.00
15-2370	Left Brace	6.30	7,051	15,000	15,000	0.0	$0.00

Figure 8-11. Safety-stock setting determination: *See the Required Safety Stock.*

This report reflects your kanban candidates, and the expected over-all inventory is projected to dramatically drop by $1.7 million from its current inventory levels if placed on kanban. The simulation will also reflect those items that passed the simulation but would increase inventory levels if placed on kanban. (See Figure 8-13.) It is up to the user's discretion whether these should be placed on kanban.

Key Notes

1. *Determining individual safety-stock settings for each part number is typically superior to having one safety-stock setting for all part numbers. For example, Approach 1 is able to place 24 part numbers on kanban with a safety-stock setting of 1 day and is projected to experience a reduction of inventory of $1.2 million, while Approach 2 is able to place 27 part numbers on kanban and is projected to reduce inventory by $1.7 million. (Both approaches used the same ASCII flat file of information.) More items will pass the simulation and carry far less inventory if you calculate individual safety-stock settings than if you simply apply the same safety-stock setting to all the part numbers.*

2. *Either historical usage or MRP's forward projection is used. In either case, the demand patterns must be considered representative of the degree of variability normally encountered. As a general rule, history repeats itself, but not always.*

3. *The master production schedule is used to drive the MRP explosion. Ensure that your particular MRP module does not go gross to net against the master production schedule, simply because on-hand inventory may have already been taken into consideration.*

4. *This tool, like all other techniques covered in this book, needs to be tested rigorously to ensure that it will serve the needs of the environment. After testing, apply it manually to a pilot area, study the results, program it if it meet your needs, and test the program rigorously to ensure it functions as designed.*

5. *You may add safety stock required for late deliveries and other issues, as required.*

Passed Simulation With Lower Inventory
Sorted by Dollar Difference

Part Number	Description	Unit Cost	Quantity On Hand	Current Dollars On Hand	Simulated Average Inventory	Simulated Dollars On Hand	Projected Inventory Change
15-2357	Left Jack	$0.58	3,000,123	$1,740,071.34	588,117	$341,107.86	($1,398,963.48)
15-2372	Lower Panel	$7.30	18,700	$136,510.00	4,765	$34,784.50	($101,725.50)
15-2370	Left Brace	$6.30	16,162	$101,820.60	3,140	$19,782.00	($82,038.60)
15-2369	Right Brace	$6.00	23,832	$142,992.00	10,659	$63,954.00	($79,038.00)
15-2366	Wedge	$55.89	453	$25,318.17	158	$8,830.62	($16,487.55)
15-2375	Upper Base	$52.87	278	$14,697.86	13	$687.31	($14,010.55)
15-2376	Rear Panel	$45.32	350	$15,862.00	41	$1,858.12	($14,003.88)
15-2364	Housing	$45.00	279	$12,555.00	97	$4,365.00	($8,190.00)
15-2374	Blade Arm	$33.76	198	$6,684.48	10	$337.60	($6,346.88)
15-2362	Stud Plate	$8.09	2,967	$24,003.03	2,348	$18,995.32	($5,007.71)
15-2359	Lower Joint with upper sleeve	$22.55	250	$5,637.50	90	$2,029.50	($3,608.00)
15-2371	Wedge Clamp	$8.00	567	$4,536.00	138	$1,104.00	($3,432.00)
15-2377	Rotor Shaft	$5.50	476	$2,618.00	31	$170.50	($2,447.50)
15-2361	Cinder Lever	$6.98	543	$3,790.14	302	$2,107.96	($1,682.18)
15-2363	Clamp	$6.00	458	$2,748.00	249	$1,494.00	($1,254.00)
15-2365	Sleeve	$1.00	444	$444.00	97	$97.00	($347.00)
15-2347	Jumper	$2.77	215	$595.55	106	$293.62	($301.93)
15-2351	Plate Jack	$2.75	125	$343.75	19	$52.25	($291.50)
15-2353	Rotor	$0.88	796	$700.48	552	$485.76	($214.72)
15-2373	Upper Panel	$4.40	57	$250.80	15	$66.00	($184.80)
15-2352	Lower Plate	$1.00	200	$200.00	18	$18.00	($182.00)

Figure 8-12. Passed simulation with lower inventory.

Passed Simulation With Lower Inventory, *continued*
Sorted by Dollar Difference

Part Number	Description	Unit Cost	Quantity On Hand	Current Dollars On Hand	Simulated Average Inventory	Simulated Dollars On Hand	Projected Inventory Change
15-2350	Jack	$7.90	66	$521.40	48	$379.20	($142.20)
15-2355	Needle	$1.00	185	$185.00	90	$90.00	($95.00)
15-2346	Left Holder	$1.00	95	$95.00	21	$21.00	($74.00)
15-2378	Front Panel	$4.58	789	$3,613.62	774	$3,544.92	($68.70)
15-2349	Splice	$0.05	3,200	$160.00	2,303	$115.15	($44.85)
15-2348	Gear	$4.50	125	$562.50	124	$558.00	($4.50)
Grand Total				**$2,247,516.22**		**$507,329.19**	**($1,740,187.03)**

Figure 8-12. Passed simulation with lower inventory (*continued*).

Passed Simulation With Higher Inventory
Sorted by Dollar Difference

Part Number	Description	Unit Cost	Quantity On Hand	Current Dollars On Hand	Simulated Average Inventory	Simulated Dollars On Hand	Projected Inventory Change
15-2358	Upper Base	$4.50	4,900	$22,050.00	47,871	$215,419.50	$193,369.50
15-2368	Pin Rod	$8.99	895	$8,046.05	1,797	$16,155.03	$8,108.98
15-2356	Stud	$9.95	120	$1,194.00	221	$2,198.95	$1,004.95
15-2354	Key	$3.50	250	$875.00	383	$1,340.50	$465.50
15-2367	Plug	$3.00	397	$1,191.00	496	$1,488.00	$297.00
15-2360	Bearing Pin	$1.00	295	$295.00	304	$304.00	$9.00
Grand Total				**$33,651.05**		**$236,905.98**	**$203,254.93**

Figure 8-13. Passed simulation with higher inventory.

Step 12: Implement Company-Owned Distribution Centers, if Applicable

Distribution centers must be set up correctly to minimize slow-moving and obsolete inventory, to avoid creating self-inflicted erratic demand patterns, and to enhance the supply-chain reaction time. If distribution centers drive the manufacturing environment, the following must be done prior to implementing kanban at the manufacturing site:

- Create and implement a stocking policy, based on volume of sales, that determines where product is stored. High-volume sales items typically should be positioned at the distribution centers. Slower-moving items should typically be stored only at the manufacturing site. By centralizing the stocking point of slow-moving items at the manufacturing site, less overall safety stock needs to be maintained. Think of it this way: Slow-moving items tend to have sporadic demand, because only a few customers typically order such items from the distributor closest to them. In order to prevent stockouts at each distribution center, each carries a fair amount of safety stock. By centralizing the stocking location, all the demand will be focused to this one location, which will tend to smooth out the demand. The smoother the demand, the lower the requirement for safety stock. The lower the safety stock, the lower the amount of slow-moving inventory that must be kept on hand, which also minimizes exposure to obsolescence.
- The distribution centers must have a consistent, agreed-upon method of calculating what should be on the shelf and what quantities are ordered.
- Downloading requirements from the distribution center to the manufacturing sites should be done daily or more often. Although shipment may take place weekly, it is necessary to provide daily downloads, in order to provide plenty of reaction time. The alternative is to carry more inventory for unexpected demand.

It is not uncommon to see each company-owned distribution center having large discrepancies between individual inventory turn ratios. The root cause has nothing to do with lead times but rather with an inconsistent determination of what should be stocked at each location, varying methods of determining how much should be on the shelf, and differences in how their respective order quantities are determined.

Step 13: Implement Manufacturing

After the company-owned distribution centers are in control, manufacturing is the next area that is implemented. Begin by leveling the production. If you do not level the production, you would create a self-inflected nonlinear demand pattern throughout the plant and supply base, leading to high levels of safety stock coupled with shortages. After the top-level build is linearized, you implement assemblies, then subassemblies, and then components.

Step 14: Implement the Supply Base

Now that the manufacturing demand patterns are smooth, we are in a position to implement the supply base. Before approaching the supply base, you should already know:

- Your expected quality levels, expected on-time delivery performance, and expected full-quantity ordered/full-quantity received levels of performance
- Who is responsible for the cost of the containers
- Who is to pay for the transportation costs of empty containers
- Your intended methodology and frequency of having the suppliers acquire their triggered orders and supplier projection
- Your goal of what the supplier lead time should be once the signal is received
- Which suppliers should carry the lead-time quantities and which should not

The contract should include the preceding terms.

Here is the sequence of implementation steps for the supply base:

1. Negotiate yearly contracts solidifying price and terms. (By the time manufacturing has implemented its top-level build items, assemblies, and subassemblies, you should have already negotiated your yearly contracts). This sets the stage to implement your suppliers onto kanban.
2. Have the kanban calculation, triggering, download capability, and supplier performance reports in place.
3. Know by supplier your current inventory levels and anticipated inventory reduction. This is charted before implementation, maintained, and acted on if there is a problem. Typical issues encountered are minimum-buy quantities are set too high and suppliers are not maintaining the lead-time quantity, as per the contract.
4. Begin implementing your suppliers. It is highly recommended that no more than two suppliers be placed on kanban at the same time, because their performance must be monitored very closely.

Consolidating the supply base is an ongoing event. Begin the implementation with your best suppliers.

Conclusion

This chapter contains fourteen steps for implementing kanban. Kanban requires support from upper level management, as there is an upfront investment to acquire containers, racks, and other needed items. To acquire the funding, there must be a reason for action and the action is tied into a cost-benefit analysis. It is unlikely that you will succeed by pursuing the design and implementation by yourself (or through your department), because kanban affects every department. Without question, success comes from the unity of all concerned as each plays a role in making kanban successful. The team is then intimately involved in a thorough design process, evaluating the environmental factors and selecting the appropriate kanban techniques. Next, you must put together a detailed implementation milestone chart, solidify costs-benefits, acquire executive approval, select kanban candidates, determine safety-stock settings, and then strategically implement kanban in one area of the business at a time.

Kanban, of all the lean manufacturing techniques, permeates every area of the business and can have serious consequences if not done correctly. Therefore, you must understand every technique that is presented and ensure that it applies to your environment before implementing. You can have an incredible kanban system that will appear to operate on its own, if it is designed for the environment and implemented correctly.

FINAL ASSEMBLY PLANNING

Master Production Schedule

A *master production schedule* reflects the final product items by time period and quantity you plan to produce. It consists of current customer orders and forecasted orders that are within capacity constraints.

Load-Smoothing

Load-smoothing is a method of developing a daily build schedule that linearizes the overall quantity of final product that is to be built each day. For example, if we were planning to build 4,800 units of Model 51A, 2,400 units of Model 51B, and 1,600 units of Model 51C in a month that had 20 manufacturing days, we would determine the daily build quantity by dividing the monthly quantity by the number of days in the given month. (See Figure A-1.) In this example, we would build 240 units of model 51A, 120 units of 51B, and 80 units of model 51C, per day.

Model	Month Build Quantity	Working Days in Month		Daily Build Quantity
51A	4,800	/ 20	=	240
51B	2,400	/ 20	=	120
51C	1,600	/ 20	=	80

Figure A-1. Creating a load-smooth schedule.

Sequencing

Sequencing is a method of refining the daily build schedule by determining the order in which the product will be produced. The objective is to create a linear cyclical demand pattern during the course of each day. There are four steps in creating a sequenced schedule.

Step 1: Determine the available production time:

9.0 hour × 60 minutes	= 540 minutes
Less 30-minute lunch	= –30 minutes
Less two 10-minute breaks	= –20 minutes
Less 10-minute clean up	= –10 minutes
	= 480 minutes available production time

Step 2: Determine the takt time: *Takt time* is the rate at which a company must produce product to satisfy customer demand. It sets the tempo to which production is synchronized. (Takt time comes from a German word that means musical beat or rhythm.)

We begin by taking the total minutes in a work day and dividing that by the daily build quantity for each model; this gives us the individual takt time for each model, as shown in Figure A-2. You can see that model 51A will be built every 2 minutes, model 51B will be built every 4 minutes, and model 51C will be built every 6 minutes. The overall takt time of the final production line is determined by dividing the 480 minutes of available production time in a day by the 440 units that are to be built each day, to equal a 1.09 minute per unit takt time. In other words, one final product will come off the production line every 1.09 minutes.

Model	Minutes in a Work Day	Daily Build Quantity	Takt Time by Product	Overall Takt Time
▲ 51A	480 Minutes	/ 240 Units	2 Minutes	**480 minutes work day**
● 51B	480 Minutes	/ 120 Units	4 Minutes	440 units produce in day
◆ 51C	480 Minutes	/ 80 Units	6 Minutes	= 1.09 min/unit takt time

Figure A-2. Determining takt time.

Step 3: Determine the lowest common denominator for each product takt times will divide into equally; 12 minutes for this example (for takt times of 2, 4, and 6 minutes). In a 12-minute period, the following will be built:

12-minute period/2 minute 51A takt time = 6 model 51As
produced in 12 minutes

12-minute period/4 minute 51B takt time = 3 model 51Bs
produced in 12 minutes

12-minute period/6 minute 51C takt time = 2 model 51Cs
produced in 12 minutes

Total: 11 units produced in 12-minute cycle

Note: Divide 12-minute cycle by 11 units = 1.09 minute per unit takt time

Step 4: Lay in the 12-minute product sequence in the most rhythmical fashion while not exceeding (6) 51As, (3) 51Bs, and (2) 51Cs.

```
=  51A   51B   51A   51C   51A   51B   51A   51C   51A   51B   51A
   ▲     ●     ▲     ◆     ▲     ●     ▲     ◆     ▲     ●     ▲
```

There will be 40 iterations (480 minutes available for production/12-minute periods) of the 12-minute period, resulting in (240) 51As, (120) 51Bs, and (80) 51Cs being produced each day.

The sequenced schedule is updated every day.

Manual Heijunka Board

The *heijunka board* is a manual method of initiating final product production, utilizing final assembly cards based on the sequence schedule. (See Figure A-3.)

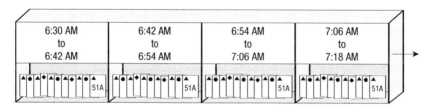

Figure A-3. Manual heijunka board.

CALCULATING KANBAN LOT SIZES

Distance in Time Required to Calculate Kanban Lot Sizes

There is a minimum length of time that should be used in gathering projected anticipated demand to calculate kanban lot sizes. This distance in time takes into consideration the longest kanban replenishment lead time and planning frequency. For example, in Figure B-1, our longest replenishment lead-time item is 2 weeks. The distance in time required to calculate kanban lot sizes would be the planning frequency of 1 week plus two times the longest replenishment lead time of 2 weeks, which equals 5 weeks. This means that we would gather a total of 5 weeks of anticipated demand going into the future, so we can then divide that by the number of days in 5 weeks to determine the average daily demand. The rationale is as follows: If a kanban were to trigger just before the end of week 1, it would take 2 weeks before it was received. That kanban would be meant to cover the demand of the following 2 weeks if the triggered order quantity is for a full kanban lot size.

Simulations

Simulation routines are used to calculate kanban lot sizes, test the kanban lot sizes against projected demand to ensure that a stockout will not occur, and determine the quantities and time periods when kanban will be triggered by part number. There is a simulation routine for each kanban container option. The following sections cover the single container discrete simulation and multiple container simulation.

Single Container Discrete Simulation

When the total of an items on hand and on order falls below the kanban lot size, a kanban order is triggered for the difference. For

Distance in Time Required to Calculate Kanban Lot Sizes

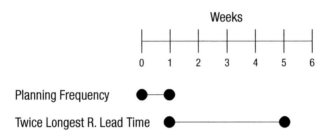

Example: 1 Week Planning Frequency, 2 Weeks Longest Kanban
Replenishment Lead Time = 5 Weeks

Figure B-1. Distance in time required to calculate kanban lot sizes.

example, if the kanban lot size is 100 and there are 70 pieces on hand and 20 pieces on order, the difference of 10 pieces will be triggered. The single container discrete simulation is demonstrated in Figure B-2. After all the data has been posted to the simulation by the system, the preliminary kanban lot size will be calculated. The 10 days of demand will be added (876 pieces), and then divided by the 10 days in time it took to gather the daily demand, which equaled an average daily demand rounded up to 88 pieces per day. The average daily demand is then multiplied by the total of a 3-day replenishment lead time and 1 day of safety stock to equal a preliminary kanban lot size of 352 pieces. The simulation will then apply the 365 pieces of on-hand inventory to the November 1, 2007, demand of 146 pieces, leaving 219 pieces in KB1. The simulation will add the 219 pieces left on hand to those on order (zero) to equal 219 pieces, and then compare that to the preliminary kanban lot size of 352 pieces. It will then trigger an order for the difference of 133 pieces (see the Simulated Trigger column). This simulation will continue all the way down to Day 10, and if a stockout does not occur, the program will accept the preliminary kanban lot size of 352 as the final kanban lot size. The system will then place the simulated trigger quantities by their respective time periods to MRP's Planned Order Release row. The system would then add up

Kanban Simulation

Part Number: 80
Description: Order Lever
Parts Grid Row Number: 3
Item Container Option: 1-Single Discrete
Start KB1: 365

On Hand Quantity: 365
Average Daily Demand: 88
Replenishment Lead: 3

Safety Stock: 1
MDays: 10

Simulation Try Number: 1

Preliminary Kanban Lot Size: 352

	Date	Demand	KB1 Ending	KB2 Ending	Download On Order due	Trigger Due	Total Received	Simulated Trigger	Total Simulated Orders Outstanding	Ending On Hand
1	11/1/07	146	219	N/A	0	0	0	133	133	219
2	11/2/07	0	219	N/A	0	0	0	0	133	219
3	11/5/07	146	73	N/A	0	0	0	146	279	73
4	11/6/07	0	206	N/A	0	133	133	0	146	206
5	11/7/07	146	60	N/A	0	0	0	146	292	60
6	11/8/07	0	206	N/A	0	146	146	0	146	206
7	11/9/07	146	60	N/A	0	0	0	146	292	60
8	11/12/07	146	60	N/A	0	146	146	146	292	60
9	11/13/07	0	60	N/A	0	0	0	0	292	60
10	11/14/07	146	60	N/A	0	146	146	146	292	60

Highest on hand stock level 219 observed on MDay 1. Lowest on hand stock level 60 observed on MDay 5. Average on hand stock level 122. Final lot size 352.

Figure B-2. Single container discrete simulation.

the *downloaded on order due quantities* (kanban orders that were triggered on the floor before the simulation) if they exist and place this total quantity in the first time period (e.g., 11/1/2007) of MRP. If a stockout occurs after replenishment lead time in the simulation, the preliminary kanban lot size will be raised by the user's setting (e.g., 10 percent) and the simulation will be rerun until it passes. If the stockout occurs within lead time (timing issue), the simulation for this part number will stop and accept the preliminary kanban lot size as the final kanban lot size. It will then generate an exception report for user intervention. (See Chapter 3 for more information on how to handle a failed simulation.)

Multiple Container Simulation

Although the multiple container option goes through a simulation, a simulation report is not generated. Simply stated, some part numbers may have dozens, if not hundreds, of containers. What is demonstrated here is how to perform the simulation. There will be two examples. The first is when the preliminary kanban lot size is higher than the old final kanban lot size, requiring the program to add containers. (See Figure B-3.) The second example demonstrates how to perform the simulation when subtracting containers when the newly calculated preliminary kanban lot size is less than the old kanban lot size, necessitating the subtracting of containers. (See Figure B-4.)

Adding Containers

The system acquires the MRP data and required fields and then inserts it into the simulation routine, as shown in Figure B-3. Next, the simulation routine is aware that there are 4 containers in play (see Old Number of Containers on the simulation report—these are still in play) and that there are 210 pieces on hand with a standard container size of 75 pieces (multiple), and 150 pieces have been downloaded as being triggered and due on November 2, 2007. Based on the on-hand inventory and the multiple-container quantity, the simulation lays in the full containers in the back, beginning

Kanban Simulation

	Part Number:	3911
	Description:	Holder
	Parts Grid Row Number:	5 – Multiple
	New Number of Containers:	5

Old Number of Containers:	4
On Hand Quantity:	210
Average Daily Demand:	88
Replenishment Lead:	3

Safety Stock:	1
Minimum:	0
Multiple:	75
Kanban Lot Size:	375

	Date	MRP Net Demand	KB1 Ending	KB2 Ending	KB3 Ending	KB4 Ending	KB5 Ending	KB6 Ending	Download On Order Due	Trigger Due	Total Received	Simulated Trigger	Total Simulated Outstanding	Ending On Hand
	Begin		0	60	75	75	—	—						210
	Trigger Add						0					75	75	
1	11/1/2007	146	0	0	0	64	0	—	0	0	0	150	225	64
2	11/2/2007	0	75	75	0	64	0	—	150	0	150	0	225	214
3	11/5/2007	146	0	68	0	0	0	—	0	0	0	150	375	68
4	11/6/2007	0	0	68	75	75	75	—	0	225	225	0	150	293
5	11/7/2007	146	0	0	0	72	75	—	0	0	0	150	300	147
6	11/8/2007	0	75	75	0	72	75	—	0	150	150	0	150	297
7	11/9/2007	146	75	75	0	0	1	—	0	0	0	75	225	151
8	11/12/2007	146	0	5	75	75	0	—	0	150	150	150	225	155
9	11/13/2007	0	0	5	75	75	0	—	0	0	0	0	225	155
10	11/14/2007	146	0	0	0	9	75	—	0	75	75	150	300	84

Highest on hand stock level 297 observed on Mday 6. Lowest on hand stock level 297 observed on Mday 6. Lowest on hand stock level observed on Mday 1. Average on hand stock level 163. Final kanban lot size 375.

Figure B-3. Multiple container simulation—add containers.

Kanban Simulation

Part Number: 3911
Description: Holder
Parts Grid Row Number: 5 – Multiple
New Number of Containers: 4

Old Number of Containers: 6
On Hand Quantity: 200
Average Daily Demand: 50
Replenishment Lead: 3

Safety Stock: 1
Minimum: 0
Multiple: 50
Kanban Lot Size: 200

	Date	MRP Net Demand	KB1 Ending	KB2 Ending	KB3 Ending	KB4 Ending	KB5 Ending	KB6 Ending	Download On Order Due	Trigger Due	Total Received	Simulated Trigger	Total Simulated Outstanding	Ending On Hand
	Begin		0	0	50	50	50	50						200
	Eliminate		X	X										
1	11/1/2007	100	—	—	0	0	50	50	0	0	0	100	100	100
2	11/2/2007	0	—	—	0	0	50	50	100	0	0	0	100	100
3	11/5/2007	80	—	—	0	0	0	20	0	0	0	100	200	20

Figure B-4. Multiple containers—subtract containers.

with container KB4, and works forward toward KB1, as reflected in the Begin row. For example, 210 pieces on hand less 75 for container KB4 leaves 135 pieces. Then, subtracting another 75 pieces for container KB3 from the 135 pieces leaves 60 pieces, which are placed in KB2. This leaves zero on hand for KB1. Both KB1 and KB2 had their containers triggered and are shown in the Download on Order Due column. Multiple containers are triggered the moment they are accessed for parts. This is the beginning position, and it reflects the exact position of the shop floor.

The next step of the simulation is to calculate the preliminary kanban lot size, which is determined by adding up MRP net demand and dividing the total by the number of manufacturing days of demand. This equals the average daily demand that is multiplied by the total of replenishment lead time and safety stock. In this example, the preliminary kanban lot size equals 375 pieces divided by 75 pieces per container to equal a need for a total of 5 containers. One more container needs to be added, which will become KB5 and will be placed as demonstrated in the Trigger Add row of the simulation. The multiple simulation routine has now positioned everything so that the simulation can test the calculated preliminary kanban lot size, as demonstrated. On Day 1 (11/1/2007), there is a requirement for 146 pieces: 60 pieces are taken from KB2, emptying the container; 75 more pieces are applied from KB3, triggering a container; and the balance of 11 pieces is taken from KB4, leaving 64 pieces and triggering another container. At the end of Day 1, we have simulated a trigger for 2 containers equaling 150 pieces, and we can see that we have a total simulated outstanding of 225 pieces, because KB5 was already automatically launched in the confines of the simulation routine. On 11/2/2007, there is zero demand, and KB1 and KB2 have been received. This simulation will continue all the way down to Day 10. If a stockout does not occur, the system will accept the preliminary kanban lot size as the final kanban lot size. The system will then place the simulated trigger quantity by its respective time periods in MRP's Planned Order Release row. The system would then add up the downloaded on order due quantities (kanban orders that were triggered on the floor before the simulation) if they exist and place this total quantity in the first time period (for example, 11/1/2007) of MRP. In this case, there were 150 pieces on order, and that quantity will be placed in 11/1/2007, along with the 225 pieces that were triggered on Day 1. So, for our example, the following quantities and time periods will be loaded into MRP's Planned Order Release row: 375 pieces on November 1, 2007, 150 pieces on November 5, 150 pieces on November 7, 75 pieces on November 9, 150 pieces on November 12, and 150 pieces on November 14. This emulates exactly what will be triggered at the point of use by date and quantity, and the supporting material needs to be made available on those dates.

If a stockout occurs after the replenishment lead time, the preliminary kanban lot size will be elevated by the user's setting (i.e., 10 percent) and will rerun the simulation until it passes. If the stockout occurs within the lead time (timing issue), the simulation for this part number will stop and accept the preliminary kanban lot size as the final kanban lot size, and then generate an exception report for user intervention. The MRP Net Demand will be placed in MRP's Planned Order Release row. (*Note:* See Chapter 3 for details on failed simulation.)

Subtracting Containers

The system acquires the MRP data and required fields and inserts them into the simulation routine, as shown in Figure B-4. Next, the simulation routine is aware that there are 6 containers in play (see the Old Number of Containers information on the simulation report, these are still in play), that there are 200 pieces on hand with a standard container size of 50 pieces (multiple), and that 100 pieces have been downloaded as being triggered. Based on that information, the simulation lays in the full containers in the back, beginning with container 4 and working forward towards KB1, as reflected in the Begin row. Next, the simulation calculates the preliminary kanban lot size, which equals 200 pieces, and then divides it by the standard container size (multiple) of 50 pieces, which equals 4 containers. Because there are 6 containers in play, 2 will have to be eliminated. On the shop floor, the containers that would be targeted for elimination would be the containers that were triggered, provided the replenishment has not started (if in the Manufacturing Queue File or Purchasing Hold File, they have not started). The simulation will do the same as shown in the Eliminate column, where KB1 and KB2 will be eliminated because they have been triggered. In addition, the 100 pieces that have been triggered are eliminated from the Download on Order Due column and will not be placed in MRP after the simulation, because they were not taken into consideration in performing the simulation to determine when new containers would be triggered. The simulation will commence and be performed as described in the preceding example.

- If the simulation fails outside of the replenishment lead time, the kanban lot size will be increased, the number of required containers will be recalculated, the Eliminate row and Download on Order column will be adjusted accordingly, and the simulation will be rerun.
- If the simulation fails within the replenishment lead time, the simulation will stop and will
  - Accept the preliminary kanban lot size as the final kanban lot size and generate an exception report for immediate user intervention
  - Place the MRP net demand in MRP's Planned Order Release row after it has been lot sized by the standard container quantity (see Chapter 3 for information on failed simulation)

If there are no containers that have been triggered and we need to subtract, we will eliminate the KB1, KB2, and so on. Once they have used their on-hand quantities, a trigger will not be made for these containers in the simulation, after the on-hand quantity is depleted.

If the simulation has passed, it will post to the MRP's Planned Order Release row by the dates the quantities triggered, as well as place the total quantity of any open triggered orders that existed prior to the simulation (as long as they are not going to be eliminated).

Simulation Exception Reports

An exception report raises a flag to the user for each kanban container option if a stockout will occur within the lead time. This is vital, because potential stockouts may be averted if action is taken immediately. The exception reports are discussed by container option.

Single Container Exception Report

This exception report is used for both the single discrete and the single full kanban container option. (See Figure B-5.) It clearly reflects the issue that on November 1, 2007, there is a demand of 400,000 expected and only 120,000 pieces are on hand.

Single Container—Order Action Required

Sorted by Vendor Number, Part Number

Part Number:	8435298
Description:	Left Jack
Component Grid Row:	12
Item Container Option:	2 Single Full
On-Hand Quantity:	120,000
Old Kanban Lot Size:	0
Replenishment Lead Time:	2
Vendor Number:	10005
Cell Number:	
Final Lot Size:	1,000,000

Day	Date	Demands	On-Order Due	KB1 Ending
1	11/01/2007*	400,000	0	−280,000
2	11/02/2007	467,000	800,000	0
3	11/05/2007	380,000	0	0
4	11/06/2007	470,000	0	0
5	11/07/2007	500,000	0	0
6	11/08/2007	540,000	0	0
7	11/09/2007	520,000	0	0
8	11/12/2007	460,000	0	0
9	11/13/2007	518,000	0	0
10	11/14/2007	490,000	0	0

Figure B-5. Single container exception report.

Dual and Triple Container Exception Reports

These container options share the same simulation routine and exception reports. For a triple container option, there are never more than two containers in-house. There are two exception reports for the dual or triple container options.

Trigger Kanban Dual and Triple Container Reports

The simulation routine is aware that both containers are in-house and that a stockout is projected to occur. How? Because nothing is on order. (See Figure B-6.) This report is informing the user that both containers are in-house and the total on-hand inventory is not enough to avert a stockout. It is telling the user to empty 1 container into the other and trigger it now. (See part number HY2785367GI.) The replenishment lead time is 3 days, there are 410

Trigger Kanban—Dual/Triple Container Report—Floor					
Sorted by Floor Location, Part Number					
Grid Row #	Part Number/ Description	Floor Location	New Kanban Lot Size	On Hand	Lead Time/ Safety
22	HY2785367GI Plug	876	652	410	3.0000 1.0000
17	2299-99878-967 Stud Plate	E532	1,300	1,050	2.0000 0.0000

Day 1 11/1/07	Day 2 11/2/07	Day 3 11/5/07	Day 4 11/6/07	Day 5 11/7/07	Day 6 11/8/07
120	400	130	0	200	160
1,500	550	580	560	550	540

Figure B-6. Trigger kanban—dual/triple container report—floor.

pieces on hand, and the stockout is projected to occur on November 2, 2007.

Dual/Triple Container Order Action Report

This simulation report is aware that 1 container has been triggered; however, a stockout will occur on November 1, 2007. (See Figure B-7.) The user needs to contact the source of supply and increase the triggered order quantity and bring it in on November 1.

Dual/Triple Container—Order Action Required

Sorted by Vendor Number, Part Number

Part Number:	13-7698
Description:	Bearing Pin
Component Grid Row:	15
Item Container Option:	3 Dual
On-Hand Quantity:	120
Old Kanban Lot Size:	200
Replenishment Lead Time:	2.00
Vendor Number:	10001
Cell Number:	
KB1 Start:	0
KB2 Start:	120
Stockout Day/Date:	1 11/01/2007
Final Lot Size:	387

Day	Date	Demands	On-Order Due	KB1 Ending	KB2 Ending
1	11/01/2007	125	0	0	0
2	11/02/2007	271	200	0	0
3	11/05/2007	75	0	0	0
4	11/06/2007	120	0	0	0
5	11/07/2007	72	0	0	0
6	11/08/2007	320	0	0	0
7	11/09/2007	0	0	0	0
8	11/12/2007	90	0	0	0
9	11/13/2007	160	0	0	0
10	11/14/2007	50	0	0	0

Figure B-7. Dual/triple container order action required report.

Multiple Container Exception Report

This report alerts the user that a stockout will occur on November 2, 2007. (See Figure B-8.) There are 900 pieces on hand, with 100 pieces due November 2. However, it is up against a demand of 1,200 by November 2. It is raising the flag for user intervention.

Part Number:	37675
Description:	Grip Handle
On-Hand Quantity:	900
Replenishment Lead Time:	3 Days
Safety Stock:	1 Day
Number of Containers:	11
Multiple:	100
Triggered Containers:	2
Stockout Day/Date:	2 11/02/2007

Day	Date	Demands	On-Order Due
1	11/01/2007	800	0
2	11/02/2007	400	100
3	11/05/2007	250	100
4	11/06/2007	50	0
5	11/07/2007	125	0
6	11/08/2007	400	0
7	11/09/2007	110	0
8	11/12/2007	75	0
9	11/13/2007	65	0
10	11/14/2007	389	0

Figure B-8. Multiple-container exception report.

KANBAN CONTAINERS, TRIGGERING, AND MAINTENANCE

Multiple Container Kanban Cards

This classic kanban approach applies three types of kanban cards for the multiple container application. These kanban cards are the production ordering card (Figure C-1), the withdrawal card (Figure C-2), and the supplier card (Figure C-3). (See Chapter 4 for details.)

Production Ordering Card		
Part Number __23470__	Description __Mach Base__	
Replenishment Work Cell Number __22__	Card: __6/8__	
Outbound Location __G5__		
Container Capacity 200 Pieces	Container Type 2S	

Figure C-1. Production ordering card.

Withdrawal Card		
Part Number __23470__	Description __Mach Base__	
Replenishment Work Cell Number __22__		
Finish Stock Location __G5__	Card: __3/6__	
Deliver Replenishment to Location __Dept 7/A6__		
Container Capacity 200 Pieces	Container Type 2S	

Figure C-2. Withdrawal card.

<table>
<tr><td colspan="2" align="center">Supplier Card</td></tr>
<tr><td>Supplier   <u>ABC Casting Corporation</u></td><td>*Delivery Cycle   <u>1-4-2</u></td></tr>
<tr><td>Time to Deliver: <u>7:00 AM, 9:00 AM, 11:00 PM, 1:00 PM</u></td><td>Card: <u>2/8</u></td></tr>
<tr><td>Part Number   <u>23460</u> ▌▌▌▌▌</td><td>Description   <u>Base Casting</u></td></tr>
<tr><td>Container Type   A6</td><td>Container Capacity   <u>200 Pieces</u></td></tr>
<tr><td colspan="2">Deliver Replenishment To Location   <u>R51</u></td></tr>
</table>

*This item must be delivered 4 times a day and the parts must be conveyed two delivery times later after the kanban is given to the supplier

Figure C-3. Supplier card.

Manufacturing Replenishment Lead Time

Manufacturing replenishment lead time is the accumulated amount of time to signal a need for replenishment to manufacturer and deliver it to the point of use. It encompasses the following elements:

- **OEMS's delay in generating a triggered kanban signal:** In the example, deduct points on the work cells using the item are placed 1 hour apart and do not register consumption immediately for a single discrete container. Delay time equals 0.125 day.
- **Manufacturing lead time:** This encompasses queue time and actual manufacturing time. In this example, the manufacturing lead time is 2 days.
- **Transport replenishment to the point of use and put away:** In this example, the transport replenishment is 1 day. Therefore, the manufacturing replenishment lead time equals 3.125 days. The manufacturing replenishment lead time is used in the kanban formula to calculate kanban lot sizes. The manufacturing lead time is used to determine the due date of the item after it has been triggered.

Purchasing Replenishment Lead Time

Purchasing replenishment lead time is the accumulated amount of time to signal a need for replenishment and to obtain and deliver it to the point of use. It encompasses the following elements:

- **OEM's delay time in generating a triggered kanban signal:** Deduct points throughout the OEM work cell are placed 1 hour apart. This impacts a single container option, in which consumption is not registered immediately. Delay time equals 0.125 day.
- **Longest interval between scheduled downloads:** The supplier agrees to download requirements; in this case, once every 2 days.
- **Supplier lead time:** The time the supplier agrees to deliver the replenishment after receiving the download; here, 2 days.
- **Maximum receiving, inspection, transport to point of use, and put-away:** In this example, 7 hours = 0.875 day.

Therefore, the purchasing replenishment lead time equals 5 days. The purchasing replenishment lead time is used in the kanban formula to calculate kanban lot sizes. The supplier lead time is used to calculate the due date of the item after it is downloaded to the supplier.

COMPANY-OWNED DISTRIBUTION CENTER CONSIDERATIONS

For those business entities that service customers through company-owned distribution centers, having a highly effective manufacturing and supply base means little if the appropriate quantities of final product are not on the shelf to satisfy customer orders.

Typical Issues

Company-owned distribution centers encountering issues will typically have symptoms of low sales order fill rates coupled with high inventories, high alternate distribution center shipment costs (because stockouts create the need for an alternate distribution center to fill the customer order), and a high lost-sales-opportunity dollar figure. The root cause(s) can stem from a variety of areas but are typically due to the following:

- Forecast is manually determined, and the changes in the market place have already taken place before the required modifications to the forecast have been made and put into effect.
- Each company-owned distribution center has its own way of determining what should be carried on the shelf.
- Each company-owned distribution center has its own way of determining when and how much to order. Even each employee from the same distribution center may have his or her own way of determining when and how much to order.
- The replenishment system at the distribution centers is push-based. When demand is projected to shift, it takes an enormous amount of effort to react to the shift in demand

in the form of order launching, realignments, and cancellations, which directly impacts manufacturing from responding properly.

Solutions

To correct the above issues, the following should be considered:
- Establish a stocking policy based upon volume sold. All distribution centers must be made aware of the stocking policy and follow it.
- Put into place a fully automated pull-based replenishment system. The application of min-max is a pull-based system—there is a calculated predetermined quantity kept on hand and consumption triggers replenishment.
- Establish the formulas that should be applied for determining quantities on the shelf and the quantities ordered. The calculations should be performed automatically. Each part number should have its own safety-stock setting, based on demand patterns.
- Automate the forecasting methodology and interface it with a simulation routine to determine anticipated date and quantity of what will be triggered, by when, for each distribution center. If using min-max, construct a min-max simulation routine.
- Automatically accumulate all the simulation output from all the distribution centers of what will be triggered by when. Automatically combine all "like" part numbers together, reflecting from an aggregate standpoint what should be required, by when. This file can automatically become input to the process of formulating the master production schedule for manufacturing.
- The triggered requirements from the distribution centers should be automated and sent electronically to the manufacturing plant daily. In implementing a fully automated replenishment system, the distribution centers are implemented first, then manufacturing, and finally the supply base.

Kanban System Design

Final Product Build Strategy

DESIGN OPTION 1: PLANNING AND INITIATING FINAL PRODUCT BUILD

☐ Kanban Technique 1: Build to a sequenced schedule _____

☐ Kanban Technique 2: Build to customer orders _____

☐ Kanban Technique 3: Combination; build to trigger kanban and customer orders _____

☐ Kanban Technique 4: Combination; build to master production schedule and customer orders _____

☐ Kanban Technique 5: Build to customer specifications on basic models _____

☐ Kanban Technique 6: Make to order _____

DESIGN OPTION 2: GENERATING THE FORECAST

☐ Kanban Technique 1: Timely ready-to-use forecast _____

☐ Kanban Technique 2: Automated forecast _____

Figure E-1. Kanban System Design

Kanban System Design

Kanban Lot Size Calculation

DESIGN OPTION 3: CALCULATING KANBAN LOT SIZES

☐ Kanban Technique 1: Synchronized Explosion™ _____

☐ Kanban Technique 2: Spreadsheet calculations _____

☐ Kanban Technique 3: Historical usage kanban calculation routine _____

Kanban Container, Triggering, and Maintenance

DESIGN OPTION 4: KANBAN CONTAINER OPTIONS

☐ Kanban Technique 1: Single discrete container _____

☐ Kanban Technique 2: Single full container _____

☐ Kanban Technique 3: Dual container _____

☐ Kanban Technique 4: Triple container _____

☐ Kanban Technique 5: Multiple container _____

Figure E-1. Kanban System Design, *continued*

Kanban System Design

DESIGN OPTION 5: MULTIPLE KANBAN CARD OPTIONS

☐ Kanban Technique 1: Classic three card _____

☐ Kanban Technique 2: Alternative two card _____

DESIGN OPTION 6: TRIGGERING

☐ Kanban Technique 1: Manual triggering _____

☐ Kanban Technique 2: Automated triggering _____

DESIGN OPTION 7: ALTERNATIVE TRIGGERING METHODS

☐ Kanban Technique 1: Broadcast methodology _____

☐ Kanban Technique 2: Material card/signal card _____

☐ Kanban Technique 3: Kanban squares _____

☐ Kanban Technique 4: Visual kanban _____

☐ Kanban Technique 5: Kanban carts _____

Figure E-1. Kanban System Design, *continued*

Kanban System Design

DESIGN OPTION 8: SYSTEM MAINTENANCE

☐ Kanban Technique 1: Manual methodology _____

☐ Kanban Technique 2: Automated methodology _____

Receiving, Inspection, Shipping, and Material Planning

DESIGN OPTION 9: ABC CLASSIFICATION APPLICATION

☐ Kanban Technique 1: ABC codes lot sizing _____

DESIGN OPTION 10: SHIPPING CONTAINER OPTION

☐ Kanban Technique 1: Reusable shipping container _____

DESIGN OPTION 11: RECEIVING OPTIONS

☐ Kanban Technique 1: Selective part count _____

☐ Kanban Technique 2: Automated count and receipt _____

Figure E-1. Kanban System Design, *continued*

Kanban System Design

DESIGN OPTION 12: INSPECTION OPTIONS

☐ Kanban Technique 1: Shopfloor inspection

☐ Kanban Technique 2: Certified suppliers

Operating Kanban in a Manufacturing Environment

DESIGN OPTION 13: MANUFACTURING CAPACITY PLANNING

☐ Kanban Technique 1: Rough-cut capacity planning

☐ Kanban Technique 2: Capacity requirements planning module

☐ Kanban Technique 3: Production line staffing

☐ Kanban Technique 4: Flexible work-cell staffing requirements

DESIGN OPTION 14: MONITORING CURRENT TRIGGERED LOAD

☐ Kanban Technique 1: Visual load monitoring

☐ Kanban Technique 2: Automated load hour monitoring

Figure E-1. Kanban System Design, *continued*

225

Kanban System Design

DESIGN OPTION 15: MANUFACTURING PRIORITIZATION

☐ Kanban Technique 1: First in, first out _____

☐ Kanban Technique 2: Sequence chart _____

☐ Kanban Technique 3: Automated availability ratio _____

☐ Kanban Technique 4: Due date _____

DESIGN OPTION 16: MATERIAL AVAILABILITY

☐ Kanban Technique 1: Visual _____

☐ Kanban Technique 2: Automated material availability simulation _____

DESIGN OPTION 17: EXPEDITING SUPPORTING MATERIAL

☐ Kanban Technique 1: Manual expedite _____

☐ Kanban Technique 2: Automated expedite routine _____

Figure E-1. Kanban System Design, *continued*

Kanban System Design

DESIGN OPTION 18: POSITIONING MATERIAL

☐ Kanban Technique 1: Point of use _____

☐ Kanban Technique 2: Overflow racks _____

☐ Kanban Technique 3: Stockroom or warehouse _____

DESIGN OPTION 19: COMMON COMPONENT PLACEMENT

☐ Kanban Technique 1: Central location _____

Kanban Technique 2: Stockroom or warehouse _____

DESIGN OPTION 20: DEDUCT POINTS AND BACKFLUSHING

☐ Kanban Technique 1: Deduct points and backflushing _____

DESIGN OPTION 21: MINIMUMS/MULTIPLES

☐ Kanban Technique 1: Minimum/multiple _____

Figure E-1. Kanban System Design, *continued*

Kanban System Design

Supply Base Kanban Integration

DESIGN OPTION 22: CONSOLIDATING THE SUPPLY BASE

☐ Kanban Technique 1: Consolidate commodity items _____

☐ Kanban Technique 2: Consolidate specialty items _____

DESIGN OPTION 23: SUPPLIER PROJECTION

☐ Kanban Technique 1: Synchronization Explosion™ supplier projection _____

☐ Kanban Technique 2: MRP gross requirements supplier projection _____

☐ Kanban Technique 3: Average daily demand projection _____

DESIGN OPTION 24: SUPPLIER LEAD-TIME QUANTITIES

☐ Kanban Technique 1: Supplier control _____

☐ Kanban Technique 2: Lead-time quantities _____

DESIGN OPTION 25: SUPPLIER INTERFACE

☐ Kanban Technique 1: Minimum/multiple _____

☐ Kanban Technique 2: Automated electronic connectivity _____

Figure E-1. Kanban System Design, *continued*

INDEX

ABOUT THE AUTHOR

 **Raymond S. Louis** is founder and CEO of Replenishment Technology Group, Inc., which specializes in supply-chain replenishment systems and lean manufacturing. He has over thirty years of hands-on experience in assessing, rectifying, designing, and implementing replenishment systems—internationally for a multitude of companies.

Raymond Louis has authored numerous trade magazine articles and is the author of two books: *Kanban for American Industry* and *Integrating Kanban with MRPII* (Productivity Press). He has taught at the University of California and California State University. He has an MBA and is certified CPIM by the American Production and Inventory Control Society and C.P.M. by the Institute for Supply Management.

Your comments, suggestions, questions, and feedback concerning this work are welcomed. Simply e-mail Raymond Louis at: *kanban@kanban.us.*

For Product Safety Concerns and Information please contact our EU
representative GPSR@taylorandfrancis.com
Taylor & Francis Verlag GmbH, Kaufingerstraße 24, 80331 München, Germany

www.ingramcontent.com/pod-product-compliance
Ingram Content Group UK Ltd.
Pitfield, Milton Keynes, MK11 3LW, UK
UKHW021825240425
457818UK00006B/71